VBQ

THE ULTIMATE

VEGAN BARBECUE

COOKBOOK

NADINE HORN & JÖRG MAYER

THE EXPERIMENT

NEW YORK

The Experiment, LLC | 220 East 23rd Street, Suite 600 | New York, NY 10010-4658
theexperimentpublishing.com

This book contains the opinions and ideas of its author. It is intended to provide helpful and
informative material on the subjects addressed in the book. It is sold with the understanding
that the author and publisher are not engaged in rendering medical, health, or any other kind
of personal professional services in the book. The author and publisher specifically disclaim
all responsibility for any liability, loss, or risk—personal or otherwise—that is incurred as a
consequence, directly or indirectly, of the use and application of any of the contents of this book.

Many of the designations used by manufacturers and sellers to distinguish their products are
claimed as trademarks. Where those designations appear in this book and The Experiment was
aware of a trademark claim, the designations have been capitalized.

The Experiment's books are available at special discounts when purchased in bulk for
premiums and sales promotions as well as for fund-raising or educational use.
For details, contact us at info@theexperimentpublishing.com.

Library of Congress Cataloging-in-Publication Data

Names: Horn, Nadine, author. | Mayer, Jörg, 1983- author.
Title: VBQ : the ultimate vegan barbecue cookbook / Nadine Horn & Jörg Mayer.
Other titles: Vegan grillen kann jeder. English
Description: New York, NY : The Experiment, LLC, 2018. | Includes index. |
Identifiers: LCCN 2017047335 (print) | LCCN 2017060630 (ebook) | ISBN
9781615194575 (ebook) | ISBN 9781615194568 (pbk.)
Subjects: LCSH: Barbecuing. | Vegan cooking. | LCGFT: Cookbooks.
Classification: LCC TX840.B3 (ebook) | LCC TX840.B3 H665 2018 (print) | DDC
641.5/636--dc23
LC record available at https://lccn.loc.gov/2017047335

ISBN 978-1-61519-456-8
Ebook ISBN 978-1-61519-457-5

Text design and photography by Nadine Horn and Jörg Mayer
Illustrations by Nessa Horn
Cover design by Sarah Smith

Manufactured in China

First printing May 2018
10 9 8 7 6 5 4 3 2 1

DEAR READERS

Hello and welcome! It's nice to have you here.

Grab yourself a cold beer—the barbecue is hot and ready.
Today we're barbecuing vegan style, and it will be a tasty experience.

Naturally, we feature barbecued tofu and seitan, but veggie lovers will certainly
get their money's worth, and we don't just mean throwing on a few zucchini
and eggplant slices. How do marinated and grilled artichokes
or a whole barbecued cabbage sound?

We've included both super simple and more elaborate recipes in this book to
satisfy not only beginners but seasoned barbecuers.

Yes, you, too, can become a vegan pitmaster.

We hope you enjoy VBQ and wish you all the best!

NADINE & JÖRG

· CONTENTS ·

· ABOUT BARBECUING ·

THE BASICS

BUYING THE RIGHT BARBECUE

The first task you have as a barbecue lover is to buy the right barbecue, and this can turn out to be an absolute ordeal of searching and hours of philosophizing about what is available on the market.

While one of your neighbors swears by gas and another will light nothing but charcoal, a third cannot understand what the fuss is about and why there is a need to have a fire anyway—an electric barbecue also does everything. The fact that this makes him the odd one out and that the other two make fun of him behind his back, fortunately, does not seem to bother him at all.

We would like to offer you advice to help you make your choice, so that you have more time to spend barbecuing.

Charcoal, gas or electric?

As we explained previously, opinions differ in this respect. Electric barbecues are easy to assemble, quick to set up, practically smoke-free and quick to dismantle. However, passionate barbecuers will scornfully criticize how impersonal electric barbecues make the process. For them, lighting a fire in a barbecue is easy, and electric barbecues are a temporary solution. But plug-in barbecues certainly have their advantages, and the most compact appliances are particularly suited to small balconies.

Gas barbecues are also quick to set up. Depending on the model, controlling the heat is possible with a push of a button, and gas-fired appliances also produce little smoke, which is why small gas barbecues are often found on the balconies of apartments. And as you cook with real fire, you'll find that word on the street is gas barbecues are definitely considered to be superior to electric barbecues. This point should not be overlooked!

But barbecuing with gas is not always the easiest thing to do. Apart from requiring space, and courage, to store gas bottles inside an apartment or house, the technology built into gas barbecues is prone to malfunctions, and they are typically expensive to clean.

The charcoal barbecuer enjoys the best reputation in the neighborhood. As the lord of the flame, he feels clearly superior to those who use gas or electricity—at least as long as he doesn't inadvertently set fire to the electric barbecuer's newly planted hedge.

Charcoal barbecues are traditional, and some believe that there simply has to be smoke when they are used. You can tell a successful barbecue from the pitmaster's smoky smell, which tends to linger on him for several days afterward.

But seriously, barbecuing for most people is associated with the ritual of lighting the fire, with the smell of glowing charcoal and, of course, the typical flavor—and we vegans are no exception.

Although charcoal barbecuing is also associated with requiring the most effort, we simply love cooking over an open flame, the primitive feeling and even all the paraphernalia that goes with it, and we can imagine that the same goes for you.

Kettle, pedestal or flat top?

If you have already decided to join the elite circle of charcoal barbecuers, you are now facing your next hurdle: the type of barbecue you should acquire. Is it really necessary to lay out good money for an expensive kettle grill, or how about a more economical flat top barbecue? Possibly even a portable one? It can be so practical, after all. And just what is a pedestal barbecue?

First and foremost, the decision you make depends on the use you are going to give it and how much you are willing to pay for it. Obviously, a small, inexpensive flat top barbecue is a practical solution if you plan to cook a few things with minimum effort by a lake. But if you are going to have a party at home, a heavy-duty appliance is more advisable.

Because of the way they are designed, pedestal barbecues should in theory be faster to make operational, given that the air passing up through the chimney-like pedestal heats up the charcoal more quickly. In practice—and after reading this book— you will find that lump charcoal or briquettes are usually lit in a special chimney starter for all types of barbecues, which eliminates this advantage. Moreover, it is more difficult to create cooking zones on a pedestal barbecue (more on that later), and many pedestal models also lack a lid, which is important for some forms of cooking.

The kettle barbecue is the perfect all-rounder. It is easy to create zones for direct and indirect cooking, the lid is an integral feature, and the temperature is very easy to control by using the top and bottom air vents.

Also, there is no need for you to dig deep into your pockets for a kettle barbecue. Good starter models with a diameter of 18 inches (47 cm) are available from about $80.

Does size really matter after all?

While it is still possible to satisfy two people using a compact picnic barbecue with a diameter of less than 12 inches (30 cm), barbecuing is much more fun when when you have more space at your disposal on the grill, especially when you have several hungry mouths to feed.

With more open space, you have the possibility of creating several different temperature zones, for food with different cooking times or to keep cooked items warm.

For parties and families, kettle grills with a diameter of 22 inches (57 cm) are recommended. But if you have little room and you are only cooking for two people, 18 inches (47 cm) is sufficient.

WHY A LID IS SO IMPORTANT

Barbecuing in its original sense means cooking food over an open fire, which does not require a lid. In fact, there is no real need for a grill when it comes to putting vegetables, tofu, etc. on a skewer and holding it over a hastily lit campfire.

But if you have a proper barbecue at your disposal and the right lid for it, new and, above all, tasty opportunities are open to you as a budding barbecue specialist.

When the lid is closed, the heat is concentrated inside the barbecue, and also on the food. Not only does this save energy, you can also create a separate zone through which fresh air circulates to act like a convection oven, allowing you to prepare dishes aside from run-of-the-mill, supermarket-bought tofu sausages. In order to have better control of the temperature inside the barbecue, it is advisable to buy a model with a lid-mounted thermometer.

WHY YOU NEED A CHIMNEY STARTER

Although charcoal barbecuers may feel superior to gas and electric barbecuers, they look enviously upon their neighbors who can instantly light up their barbecues with the press of a button.

Luckily, lighting charcoal can be sped up with the use of a chimney starter. Instead of lighting the fuel inside the barbecue, the charcoal or briquettes are packed tightly inside the chimney starter and lit from

below. The air flowing up through the chimney helps the charcoal lumps or briquettes catch fire quickly and easily.

Depending on the fuel, the charcoal becomes covered with a white ash layer in 20 to 40 minutes, and then is ready to use.

THE IMPORTANCE OF CHOOSING THE RIGHT BARBECUE TONGS

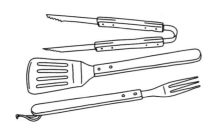

So you now have a 22-inch (57-cm) barbecue. Bear in mind that all around this space, you can feel the heat coming from the grill, which is directly heated to about 575°F (300°C).

Since the rest of the surfaces are also quite "warm," it is obvious that there is really only one thing short tongs are good for: a back scratcher.

Barbecue tongs should therefore be about 16 inches (40 cm) in length and made from stainless steel. They should also allow you to grip food with precision.

WHAT TO LOOK FOR IN A SPATULA

The same things you look for in tongs apply to the spatula. However, you should make sure that the thickness of the stainless steel at the end of the spatula is not too thick, so that it can slide easily under vegan burgers.

WHY THERE IS NO NEED FOR SPECIAL BARBECUE GLOVES

Just to clear up any misunderstanding: barbecue gloves are a sensible investment. However, the grip on the silicone gloves you can buy in the barbecue section of a hardware store soon wears out, and leather gloves are naturally out of the questions for vegans.

You can find a sensible alternative in the workwear section. There you have light, fireproof and ergonomic gloves with the perfect grip. Admittedly, they do not protect you from heat as well as barbecue gloves, but they are good protection against sparks.

WHY CLEANING UTENSILS MATTER

Understandably, you do not want to deal with the annoying task of cleaning your barbecue before using it. Nevertheless, we advise you to at least have a brass or stainless steel wire brush handy for this unloved task.

As with the tongs and spatula, the wire brush should also have a long handle because it is best to clean the grill while it is hot.

WHY YOU NEED PANS, PERFORATED TRAYS AND CONTAINERS

Without trying to give the impression that we are not keen on tofu sausages, we would like to point out that you can prepare other delicious and perhaps more exciting dishes on the barbecue.

You can prepare tasty braised dishes and sauces in cast-iron pans or pots, which in a closed barbecue will acquire a delicious smoky aroma. You can also grill small or sliced vegetables by using heat-conducting perforated trays, and stainless steel containers are an environmentally friendly alternative to aluminum.

Of course we have nothing against tofu sausages with ketchup, but who could say no to a delicious braised vegetable dish?

WHY SKEWERS DESERVE THEIR OWN SECTION

Any complete set of barbecue equipment should contain bamboo or stainless steel skewers. But you should know how to use them.

Bamboo skewers, whether the thin shish kebab skewers you keep at the back of the cutlery drawer or the thick ones, should be soaked in water for at least 30 minutes before use. Otherwise, you risk the skewers literally burning through the food. On the other hand, wet skewers produce smoke that is absorbed by the vegetables, mushrooms and tofu, giving them a delicious flavor.

Metal skewers are best used with large pieces, which need to stay on the grill for longer. Heat passes through the metal skewers, and also cooks things like cubes of winter squash or seitan from the inside.

If you have a couple of herb pots in the kitchen or you are one of the lucky ones to have your own herb garden, you can also make use of them. Sturdy sticks of rosemary or lemongrass rubbed with olive or sesame oil make excellent skewers and season the skewered food from the inside.

We also recommend that you use flat or at least angled skewers, so that the food does not rotate when you turn the skewers over.

Now you know why skewers deserve their own section.

WHY THE LITTLE THINGS MATTER

The basting brush

It is obvious that vegetables do not contain a lot of fat, and neither do tofu, tempeh or seitan, among others. Unlike carnivores, vegan barbecuers also have to take more care that food being cooked over the open fire does not dry out.

With a long enough (do you remember the section on tongs?) and flame-resistant basting brush, you can use a little oil or leftover marinade to make sure everything stays nice and juicy and delicious.

Aluminum foil and alternatives

While it is wonderful that aluminum containers can be replaced by reusable stainless steel ones, sometimes you have no choice but to use aluminum foil—for example, to make foil parcels. But we recommend you reduce your use of aluminum foil to a minimum, and not just for environmental reasons.

If aluminum foil comes into contact with an acid or salt, it can break down—and even dissolve, which is not exactly what "healthy barbecuing" is all about.

Healthy alternatives include banana leaves, which you can find at specialty food shops, and dried corn husks. Both of these also flavor the food.

Since vegetable parcels are normally cooked with indirect heat, you can also wrap them in sturdy parchment paper. It goes without saying that you have to keep a close eye on the parcels; parchment paper also tends to catch fire.

FANCY ACCESSORIES

Pizza stone

Temperatures over 575°F (300°C) can be reached in a kettle grill with a large enough lid and good air flow. Pizza lovers soon come to this conclusion: "That's hotter than my oven gets." And that means that in theory, pizza cooks faster and hotter in a barbecue, making the ideal stone oven–cooked pizza a little closer to reality.

And yes, it actually works, as long as you have the right accessories. Many barbecue manufacturers offer suitable pizza stones for their respective models, some of which can even be integrated into the grill.

Alternatively, any conventional cordierite pizza stone can be placed on the grill. You only need to take into account the size of the barbecue, as this ensures unhindered air circulation that is needed to keep the temperature inside the barbecue high. We recommend a pizza stone measuring 14 inches (36 cm) or less for a barbecue with a diameter of 22 inches (57 cm).

The pizza stone needs to be preheated for 20 minutes in a lit barbecue with the lid closed. The prepared pizza with toppings is then laid on the hot stone and baked with the lid closed at 575 to 650°F (300 to 350°C) for 4 to 6 minutes.

The Dutch oven

We could have mentioned this in the "Why you need pans, perforated trays and containers" section, but we thought that the Dutch oven deserved more attention.

Oh, you don't know what a Dutch oven is? No problem, we can explain. A Dutch oven is a heavy cast-iron pot with an equally heavy, typically flat lid. Strictly speaking, you do not need a barbecue to use a Dutch oven, as even a simple campfire will do—in fact, this is how it is traditionally used.

Many barbecue manufacturers offer Dutch ovens that are suited to their models. If you would like to use an alternative from another manufacturer, you should pay attention to the diameter.

The Dutch oven sits on the grill, and the charcoal goes around it. If your barbecue does not have a lid, you can put lumps of charcoal or briquettes directly on the lid of the pot so that it becomes really hot on the inside.

A Dutch oven is particularly suitable for making slow-cooked braised dishes and smoky stews, and for baking bread.

Cast-iron griddles and grills

Not every dish can be prepared on a wire grill. A cast-iron griddle makes a good alternative to a cast-iron pan and offers a larger surface area.

If you prefer char marks, you should consider the purchase of a cast-iron grill. These are available as standard replacements, while several manufacturers offer inserts to fit into a recess in the grill.

Cast-iron accessories need to be preheated before putting on the food. Ten minutes is usually enough with the lid closed.

Bricks

Even if you do not build your own barbecue, bricks are a sensible, versatile complement to your barbecuing equipment.

Apart from the fact that you can use them under the feet of the barbecue to give it more stability, they can also be used as skewer holders or if you want to heat food from above.

For a quick homemade skewer holder, use thin bricks, spaced apart directly on the grill. Position the skewers between the bricks so that they are not in direct contact with the grill. This is particularly recommended with soft food that would fall apart on the hot grill.

Or, to toast sandwiches and panini, place a clean brick on a hot grill and preheat it with the lid closed for 20 to 30 minutes. Then you can lay the heated brick on top of the sandwich on the grill to toast it from the top and bottom.

A flowerpot lid

If your barbecue does not come with a lid, then here is a trick you can use. An upturned terra-cotta flowerpot can be placed directly on the grill as an improvised lid for small dishes.

WHERE AND WHEN TO LIGHT A FIRE

BARBECUING AT HOME, OR HOW NOT TO ANNOY YOUR NEIGHBORS

You can theoretically barbecue on even the smallest balcony. However, as there is no such thing as the "right to barbecue," lease agreements can forbid them.

If the landlord is a barbecue enthusiast and does not forbid barbecuing in principle, that does not mean a free ticket for an all-day smokefest on the balcony.

Even if your upstairs neighbors praised your delicious, home-smoked tofu at the last meal you shared together, they will probably not be happy to have the hickory smoke from your balcony filling their apartment through the living room window.

In such cases, the fun will soon come to an end and may land the barbecuers in court. Incidentally, you also run the risk of a smoking ban if you do an inordinate

amount of smoking in the courtyard of an apartment complex or even on your own property.

Even if it is possible to barbecue with relatively low-smoking charcoal, balcony barbecuers can avoid this scenario by using electric or gas barbecues. In any case, it is a good idea to notify your neighbors of your intention to have and use a barbecue: consideration and a friendly dinner invitation can go a long way to keeping up good, neighborly relations at the best and worst of times.

BARBECUING IN THE GREAT OUTDOORS

Anyone with the romantic notion of packing the barbecue in the trunk, driving off and setting up camp amid beautiful scenery will have a hard time of it in many places.

Barbecuing in the open air can be punished by fines, many secluded meadows are privately owned, and barbecuing is strictly prohibited in nature reserves.

Many public parks have designated barbecuing areas, and only with this explicit permission is the all-clear given for barbecuing enjoyment.

Naturally, as responsible barbecuers, we take all our garbage home, including the leftover charcoal, and dispose of it ourselves.

WHAT TO DO OUTSIDE OF THE BARBECUING SEASON

According to hard-core barbecuers, there is no such thing as the wrong weather, only the wrong clothes. But seriously, every season of the year has its "barbecue occasion."

While our smoky chili cooked in a Dutch oven on page 127 is of course wonderfully suited to cold winter evenings, winter vegetables cooked on the barbecue are also delicious.

It goes without saying that you will need to warm up during the colder months of the year. However, the additional layer of clothing you wear should not put you in any danger. Please refrain from wearing scarves, jackets and hats made from highly flammable fabrics.

WHAT MAKES THE BEST FIRE IN A CHARCOAL BARBECUE

LUMP CHARCOAL OR BRIQUETTES?

Although it is completely possible, few barbecue enthusiasts would light their barbecues using wood they have cut themselves or bought, and instead will reach for charcoal or briquettes, which are readily available, to which they are enticed in the same way small children are drawn to the sweets at a supermarket checkout counter.

But what should you buy and what special offers should you go for?

Charcoal

Charcoal is, as its name implies, essentially charred wood, from which moisture is removed by the process of charcoal burning. So it burns longer and hotter than its raw material.

However, the craft of charcoal burning is dying out. Traditional charcoal, which is now sold for barbecues, is almost exclusively produced by an industrial process and mostly imported. If you value locally produced, then it is quite difficult to find. Only a few manufacturers use timber felled exclusively to produce lump charcoal and briquettes. You should seek advice about what is the best on the market. Some companies even process waste from furniture production, which is very admirable.

By the way, you can tell a good sack of charcoal from the noise it makes when you shake it a little. If the contents make a clinking sound, it indicates that there are large pieces and therefore good quality charcoal.

Briquettes

Charcoal briquettes are mostly made of compressed charcoal dust and starch. They do not burn as hotly as charcoal, and the process of lighting them takes longer. They

also glow for a longer time and are suitable for large barbecue events and for food that needs slow braising on the grill.

HOW TO AVOID EXCESS SMOKE

The expression a "smoky flavor" actually sounds as if what is good about barbecuing is smoke. While this is certain, it is not even the half of it.

Although completely smoke-free cooking is not possible with conventional charcoal barbecues, food can still be given the typical barbecued flavor even with little or no visible smoke.

Heavy smoke, however, which usually occurs when lighting the barbecue, is a disturbance, has nothing to do with developing flavors, and fortunately can be avoided.

The development of smoke often depends on different factors. Charcoal of inferior quality with a high dust content produces more smoke than a good quality charcoal. The same is true of briquettes.

Poor fire starters often produce smoke and lead to the neighbors' view being obscured. The use of a good starter can prevent or at least minimize smoking.

HOW TO LIGHT A FIRE

The barbecue has been set up; the sack of charcoal is also ready. You put charcoal inside the barbecue, take out a match and go, right?

It is actually not so easy to get this fuel to burn. Every summer you see barbecue enthusiasts with red faces puffing away at a tiny flame in the hope that it grows into a full-blown fire.

It is much simpler to use a chimney starter, which we have already looked at in "The basics." Just have a few firelighters and a cigarette lighter or match at the ready, and nothing else is needed; shortly you will have the barbecue at a temperature at which it is ready to use.

BUYING FIRELIGHTERS

First take the bottle of alcohol . . . and put it far away from the barbecue. Lighter fluids have no place near a grill or any kind of fire.

There are enough safe and eco-friendly alternatives on the market, with the simple, low-smoke, natural firelighters made of wood shavings preferable to paraffin cubes.

If you are a bit more experimental, in the barbecue department of hardware stores you will also find gas torches and air blowers, although the latter causes sparks to fly and should on no account be used in the immediate vicinity of your wooden garden shed, unless you were thinking of having it demolished anyway.

MAKING YOUR OWN FIRELIGHTERS

It is an advantage here if you are good with your hands, because you can quickly and easily make your own firelighters with untreated wood chips and leftover candle wax. Effective upcycling.

To do this, pack the wood chips tightly into the cavities of a silicone ice cube tray, for instance, and pour the melted candle wax over the top. Leave them for a little while to harden, and then pop the cubes out of the mold. And there you have safe firelighters at the ready, made from things that would have ended up being thrown out.

If this is too complicated for you, take yesterday's newspaper, crumple up a few sheets and use them as a firelighter. However, this process may have to be repeated as paper burns more quickly than the time it takes for charcoal to catch fire. There is always a catch.

THE PROPER WAY TO HANDLE A CHIMNEY STARTER

Fill the top compartment with charcoal or briquettes. For a large amount, you may have to add a firelighter to the compartment.

Away from the wind, stand the starter on a fire-resistant surface, such as a sufficiently thick steel plate, or directly on the grill.

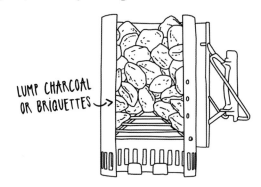

LUMP CHARCOAL OR BRIQUETTES →

ABOUT BARBECUING

Put a few firelighters or crumpled sheets of newspaper under the starter, light them, and wait for 20 to 30 minutes. When the charcoal is coated with a white ash layer, it is ready to be put into the barbecue. Don't forget to wear your new fireproof gloves.

HOW TO CONTROL THE HEAT IN A BARBECUE

GETTING TO THE RIGHT TEMPERATURE

Light up the coals, tip them into the barbecue, put on the food and that's it.

Right? No. Wrong! Totally wrong!

Before you lay the food on the grill, you are faced with the challenge of keeping the embers lit and bringing the barbecue to the correct temperature at which vegetable skewers and tofu will cook.

As a rule, with simple flat top barbecues you only have a few options and tools at your disposal. The main thing is to get enough oxygen to the coals. To put this as simply as possible, this means blowing carefully to increase the heat, and reducing the amount of charcoal to cool the barbecue down. The coals you take out should be put into another heatproof container so that they can be returned to the barbecue as required.

Pedestal and kettle grills have more sophisticated options for controlling the supply of air. The air intake vent is found below, and this is usually controlled by means of a turning mechanism. Models with lids have an adjustable exhaust vent. In a nutshell, the more air flowing through the barbecue, the hotter it will become.

The thermometer in the lid only shows how hot the entire cooking area is, while the temperature directly over the grill can only be gauged by experience or by putting your hand over it. Although it sounds painful, there is no need to worry. Hold your hand about 4 inches (10 cm) above the grill and start counting. If you have a functioning pain threshold (and we certainly hope you do), you will instinctively pull your hand away after a certain time. The seconds (yes, this should only take a few seconds) you count allow you to work out the approximate temperature.

If you pull your hand away after 1 to 2 seconds, then the grill will have reached a temperature of about 575°F (300°C) or above.

If your instinct kicks in after 5 to 7 seconds, then it is about 200°F (100°C) lower, and if you can leave your hand over the grill for more than 10 seconds, you can cook at a low temperature of about 250°F (120°C).

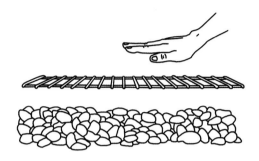

KEEPING THE RIGHT TEMPERATURE

If you open the air intake vents fully, you will be cooking on high, and that is never a good thing. The delicious skewers directly over the embers will turn black before the vegetables even have the chance to cook.

In this case, the bottom vents should be closed somewhat. By decreasing air flow, the heat is reduced.

In order to prevent the entire grill surface from becoming too hot, you should set up different cooking zones at the beginning. This way you will have a hot, direct cooking surface and a cooler, indirect cooking zone. You can find out how to do this in the next section, "Different cooking methods."

WHEN TO PUT THE FOOD ON THE GRILL

Even when you have a full understanding of the need to wait a little after lighting the coals before putting the first skewer on the grill, you also have to give the grill some time to heat up, particularly if you want char marks.

The easiest way to do this is with a lid that keeps the heat inside the barbecue and close to the grill.

This principle is even more important when using certain accessories. As previously explained, a pizza stone has to heat up if you want a crispy pizza crust. You should leave it undisturbed for at least 20 minutes in a closed barbecue.

Cast-iron grills and griddles store heat particularly well. This also means that they need time to heat up.

It should be enough to leave them for 10 minutes over a high heat with the lid closed.

DIFFERENT COOKING METHODS

DIRECT COOKING

We come back to the notion of "light up the coals, tip them into the barbecue, put on the food and that's it."

While this may have sounded simple, it actually isn't. Direct cooking means, first of all, laying the food directly over the embers and cooking it for a short time over high heat. That is quite okay for tofu sausages and seitan steaks, and even vegetables can be roasted over direct heat as long as they finish cooking at a lower temperature. You will always have to set up a direct cooking surface—there always has to be somewhere to put the coals.

Especially in the case of picnic barbecues, there is really no choice but to cook directly, given that there is little space on the charcoal grate over which to distribute the embers. You have to realize that it will be difficult to prepare dishes requiring a longer cooking time, and also to smoke food. You also have to be ready to turn the food over at the right moment, otherwise you will end up with a plate full of charred remains.

INDIRECT COOKING

Direct and indirect cooking. It would be lovely to speak philosophically of yin and yang. Of course, this does not apply, because the two methods are not complete opposites. Both require fire and heat, but indirect—as its name suggests—needs less.

Indirect cooking actually means cooking "next to the embers"—in other words, with the heat released by the charcoal or briquettes on the side. But this should not be taken too literally; the food is naturally placed on the same grill, just not directly over the fire.

This method works quite well with barbecue models with lids, because the food is cooked in an enclosed space with heat from all sides.

The following section offers a few options that enable you to cook indirectly.

TWO-ZONE COOKING

The simplest version. The glowing coals are tipped into only one side of the barbecue after lighting. One half of the charcoal grate is left empty. You can cook directly over the left side and indirectly over the right side. Simple, practical and reliable.

THREE-ZONE COOKING

If you prefer, the surface of the grill can be divided into three zones, with two different direct-cooking zones, one with a higher heat and the other with a slightly lower heat. Simply use different amounts of charcoal. The more charcoal you use, the higher the heat.

RING ARRANGEMENT

The problem with zone cooking is the fact that the heat distribution overlaps in the middle of the barbecue. This is because the air intake is usually found at the bottom of the barbecue, and also because the coals burn unevenly. The heat is boosted by fresh air in the middle, while less happens around the edges.

With the ring method, the air blows freely through the middle part of the barbecue, and the charcoal or briquettes burn more evenly inside.

This means that the coals are only spread around the edge of the charcoal grate. Direct cooking takes place on the outside, while the inside zone is for indirect cooking. This only really works well with kettle barbecues.

THE DEATH STAR

The Death Star method is not only for *Star Wars* fans, although we will spare you an explanation of the name. Let us just say it is a private joke. Film buffs will catch the significance of this sooner or later.

This method involves placing an aluminum container in the middle of the barbecue. As it is reused, no waste is produced. Coals or briquettes are placed to the left and right of it.

Now you have the possibility of cooking directly on the sides of the grill, keeping a large space free in the middle where you can cook dishes to perfection.

However, this method only works with barbecues whose air intake is not fully concealed underneath. Several manufacturers offer accessory char-baskets that can be placed on the sides inside the barbecue to create the same effect. This also makes cleaning easier.

Bonus tip

If you fill the container with water, the steam produced will keep the food moist, especially with the lid closed.

SMOKING

WHAT "SMOKING" ACTUALLY MEANS

Smoking is one of the oldest methods of food preservation. Since the invention of the refrigerator, there is no longer any need to store smoked food in the living room (it smells delicious, but there is only so much you can take), and food is smoked almost exclusively to give flavor. And this is enough reason to address the subject in a little more depth; you can trust us on that one.

With a fire in the barbecue and a lid to create an enclosed space, you have the perfect conditions for smoking. At least for hot smoking.

WHAT VEGANS CAN SMOKE

Basically anything you can put on the barbecue can be smoked. However, we must admit that the aroma of the various types of wood do not suit all foods.

Of course, tofu, seitan and tempeh are very suitable, and these products are readily available.

But different vegetables are also ideal for smoking. For instance, green asparagus tastes fantastic with a subtle aroma of apple or beechwood, and slowly smoked eggplant halves can tolerate the strong aroma of hickory.

WHAT TO SMOKE WITH

Hardware stores and online retailers have a huge selection of different sorts of smoking wood chips. Coarse wood chips are practical and easy to handle, and they store well.

If smoking with store-bought wood chips gets boring after a while, you can experiment with making them yourself from well-dried wood. The only important thing to remember is to use untreated wood. So do not cut up old varnished chairs and hope for a delicious aroma.

You should also try cooking on grilling planks. These are available in different varieties and can be  purchased at many hardware stores. We insist you try our large herb-filled onions cooked on a grilling plank (see page 121).

WHAT NOT TO SMOKE WITH

It may come as a shock to some people, but no, tofu sausages should never be smoked or grilled over pine cones, because the burning cones produce carcinogenic substances.

Otherwise, as mentioned, only untreated, seasoned wood should be used for smoking.

HOW TO HOT SMOKE FOOD

Having gone over the theory, we now come to the practice.

Before you light the barbecue, you have to soak the smoking wood chips for at least 30 minutes in plenty of water, otherwise they will burn instead of producing smoke.

Drain the chips well and spread them over the glowing coals. The food to be smoked is placed on the indirect cooking side of the barbecue and the lid is closed. A handful of chips is enough to produce 15 to 20 minutes of intense smoke. You can then test to see whether there is sufficient flavor, or whether you need to refill the barbecue with chips. There is nothing more to it.

Alternatively, you can purchase a smoker box and fill it with the soaked wood chips. This goes directly over the heat source. So you can also smoke in a gas

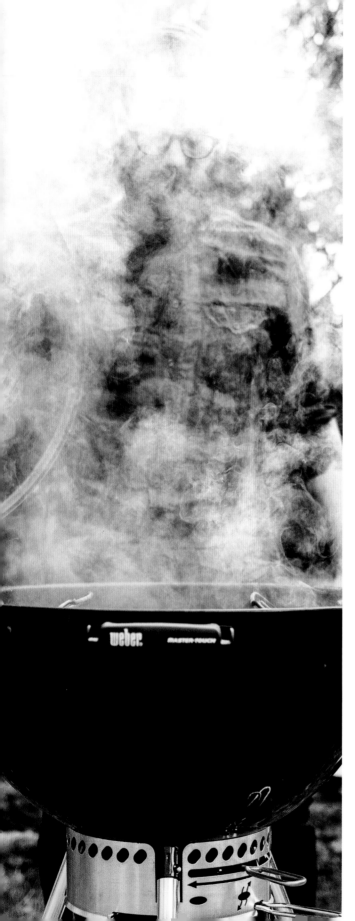

barbecue. Not only does smoking make food taste delicious, it is also extremely easy.

Grilling planks should be soaked for about an hour. The plank is used with indirect heat on a preheated grill. As soon as it starts to smoke, the food is placed directly on the plank and the lid is closed. Grilling planks can be reused time and time again, so do not discard them; soak them again and keep on smoking.

Bonus tip

You can also soak smoking chips in other liquids. While beer and red wine are obvious choices, soaking wood in apple or grape juice adds a wonderful flavor. Adding some rum to the soaking water will give the food the aroma of caramel.

CLEANING THE BARBECUE

WHY THE BARBECUE SHOULD BE CLEANED

Firstly, let us disprove a persistent rumor: baked-on leftovers from the last five barbecuing seasons do not improve the flavor of barbecued food!

The large amounts of grease, food remains and dust sticking to a grill do not give seitan steaks or veggie burgers more decorative char marks.

So if you do not want to deal with the—admittedly annoying—task of cleaning for reasons of hygiene, then at least do it for the sake of your char marks. People also eat with their eyes.

THE BEST WAY TO CLEAN AND CARE FOR YOUR BARBECUE

Unfortunately, there is no such thing as a maintenance-free, self-cleaning barbecue, so it is up to the pitmaster to make sure that the equipment looks good and works well for years to come.

First of all, the grill requires a little attention before and after use. There is no need to worry; the cleaning will be done in a jiffy if the right method is used.

Cleaning

It is best to clean the grill while it is hot. While it would seem natural to leave the cleaning until after barbecuing, this step can also be undertaken while the barbecue is heating up, before the food is laid on the grill. We actually recommend cleaning be done both before and after. Doing it after cooking will clean the initial food residue, and doing it again before the next barbecuing session will ensure a clean surface for your new food.

Heat the grill to a high temperature, and then use a long-handled wire barbecue cleaning brush (see page 13) to give it a good clean until the metal bars have recovered their sheen. Then turn the grill over, if possible, and clean off any food residue from the underside. Turn the grill back over to its correct position and wipe it with a cloth soaked with vinegar. You can use clean and finely burned ash from inside the barbecue as an abrasive for polishing. Use a cloth for this final cleaning step, but hold it with tongs, otherwise it can be painful and your cookout will come to an end sooner than you had planned.

If the grill is very dirty and cannot be cleaned with hard scrubbing, you can wrap it in a couple of sheets of damp newspaper (perhaps left over from the kindling) and leave it overnight. The moisture will soften the stubborn dirt, which will be so much easier to remove the next time you use the barbecue. There is certainly no need for chemical cleaners.

Care

Every now and then you need to devote some time to the barbecue itself. This should be done when it is cold. The charcoal grate also needs cleaning from time to time, and it does not hurt to wipe down the inside of the barbecue with a damp cloth. Aluminum or stainless steel drip pans and char-baskets can also be wiped down occasionally, if only to remove any unsightly rust stains.

Apart from that, it is obvious that your barbecue is not happy to spend the entire year outdoors. Bring it into the living room! Even though you obviously won't be lighting it up inside, you can at least enjoy the sight of it on rainy days. At least, if that's your thing. Who knows?

We are joking, naturally. It does the barbecue's metal frame a world of good if it can stay dry inside the house or in a shed over the winter.

But if for reasons of space it has to stay outside or it is given a space in a damp basement or in the garage, you are well advised to think about getting a cover for your barbecue. Manufacturers usually offer these as an accessory, or alternatively, you can make do with a tarp and some string.

Bonus tip

Of course, very capable pitmasters delegate the cleaning and maintenance tasks to their guests. After working off their meal, they can now sit back with a well-deserved beer.

SAFETY

FINDING THE BEST PLACE FOR A BARBECUE

Although it should be quite apparent, nevertheless barbecues cause fire damage to their owners' and even neighboring properties year after year.

Therefore, to clear up any misconceptions: barbecues must be set up in such a way that any flying sparks or heat buildup cannot start a fire. This means that the shady place near the hedge that has been dried out by the summer heat definitely is not appropriate.

A barbecue also has no place next to your store of kindling or the compost heap.

Moreover, the barbecue must have a secure footing. Particularly economical models unfortunately tend to have wobbly legs. If the slightest gust of wind makes the barbecue creak and wobble, it should be moved quickly to a more sheltered spot.

In this new place the barbecue will withstand sudden storms, but certainly not the weight of a child, who is capable of mistaking the handle for a pull-up bar. Therefore, never leave children and pets unsupervised near a hot barbecue!

LIGHTING THE BARBECUE SAFELY

As explained on page 18, the barbecue can be safely lit with firelighters made from wood shavings or newspaper. Alcohol has no place here as a firelighter, and even if there were no problems the first twenty

times, there is no guaranteeing a safe twenty-first time. The escaping vapors (and those coming from the wet charcoal) can burst into flame and start a fire. Not exactly the best way to open the barbecuing season.

Even if you feel like a bit of an adventurer in the wilderness while barbecuing in your newly purchased all-weather jacket, it has no place near a fire. While a cotton shirt will just burn to a crisp, in an extreme case, the synthetic fabric will melt, leaving you not only in flames, but forever joined to your beloved jacket. One wonders whether it is a good thing to feel so strongly about a piece of clothing.

PUTTING OUT THE BARBECUE

Water puts out a fire; that much is clear. However, it is not advisable to pour a whole bucket of water over the embers, because glowing embers can be hurled out of the barbecue and continue to burn. So it is better to pour water over them gradually and carefully to put them out.

Barbecues with lids are even easier and safer to put out, by simply cutting off the source of oxygen that keeps them lit. To do this, completely close all the vents, put on the lid and wait. The last coal will smolder and eventually completely extinguish.

DO NOT POUR LIQUID OVER GLOWING EMBERS

Even if it cannot be completely avoided at the end of a party, liquid should not be poured over the glowing embers, apart from the water used to put them out, especially marinades and sauces. The smoke that is inevitably produced carries the carcinogenic benzopyrene from the coals to the food being cooked, and it tends to linger.

Since a marinade is not meant for eating, it should be drained off completely before putting the food on the grill. You can also brush vegetable skewers with additional marinade as they are cooking, but then they should be laid over a drip tray.

AVOID BURNED FOOD

Although this observation is not always shared, there is a difference between "deliciously golden brown" and "black as a briquette." And this does not apply only to the color, but also to your health.

The carbon that adheres to burned food is not actually unhealthy, but depending on the degree of charring, this will also result in polycyclic aromatic hydrocarbons, acrylamide and heterocyclic amines.

Always pay attention to what you are cooking, and if it needs to cook longer, finish it off over indirect heat. It will also taste better.

ASH DISPOSAL

Highly contaminated ashes—after cooling, naturally—should be disposed of as general waste. Clean ashes, which is biochar left behind by burning charcoal made from domestic wood stocks, are recyclable and suitable as plant fertilizer. But less is more. If you have no need for fertilizer, put the ashes on your compost heap or dispose of them as organic waste.

· HOW TO BARBECUE VEGAN STYLE ·

THE RIGHT WAY TO BARBECUE VEGETABLES

Vegetables can taste really good, but you already know that. Nonetheless, there are a few things you need to consider when it comes to barbecuing vegetables, so you can be certain that only properly cooked and delicious vegetables end up on your plate, because "throwing them on the grill and waiting" is not quite the way to do it. We have put together a few tips for different varieties of vegetables.

MARINATING AND SALTING

The simplest form of preparation is also the most popular. With a simple marinade comprising only a quality oil and salt, you can make delicious barbecued vegetables to serve as a side dish or garnish.

Zucchini and eggplant

Both vegetables can be prepared by halving and slicing, salting well and leaving them to stand. The salt draws out the excess water from the zucchini and eggplant. After rinsing the pieces well under running water, you can lightly season them with fresh thyme, brush them with olive oil and lay them on the grill.

Thin zucchini slices need about 6 minutes each side over indirect heat; score the cut side of eggplant halves in a crisscross pattern, grill over direct heat for 3 minutes until the flesh is lightly roasted and cook over indirect heat with the lid closed for another 20 to 30 minutes.

Squash

Both red kuri (Hokkaido) and butternut squash are particularly good vegetables for barbecuing. Cut the squash into wedges 1½ inches (4 cm) thick, then season

with salt, pepper, a little nutmeg and olive oil, and grill over direct heat for 2 minutes each side.

Then place the wedges over indirect heat, close the lid and cook for another 10 minutes.

Peppers

Cut peppers into large pieces, season with salt and olive oil, and grill them on their skin side over high heat. The skin should be allowed to char, which will make it easy to peel and give the flesh a delicious roasted aroma.

If you like your peppers crispy, this will only take a few minutes. If you like your peppers a little softer, leave them on a lower heat for about 10 minutes.

Asparagus

Green asparagus tastes wonderful when grilled. In order to preserve their delicious aroma, brush the spears with plenty of olive oil and lay them (preferably in a perforated container) on the grill over direct heat. The spears only need about 90 seconds. Then they will still be crispy but with lovely char marks and a smoky aroma.

After cooking, season them with coarse sea salt, coarsely ground pepper and lemon zest.

For something a little more elaborate, there is a recipe for barbecued asparagus with pepper dressing on page 115.

Beets

Coat whole, unpeeled beets with olive oil and put them on the grill. Cook over indirect heat with the lid closed for 25 to 30 minutes, turning them over often.

When they can be pierced relatively easily to the center with the tip of a knife, they are ready and can be taken out. After cooling a little, the charred skin will peel off easily.

Season the peeled beets with a little salt, pepper and finely chopped fresh dill or another fresh herb such as parsley or chives.

BLANCHING

Some vegetables give better results if they are briefly blanched before cooking. The flavor of marinades and seasonings are better absorbed by the vegetables and the cooking time is shorter, so that the vegetables make it to your plate while still crispy, before being burned to a crisp.

Broccoli and cauliflower

Cut the broccoli and cauliflower into florets and blanch in abundant salted water for 5 minutes. Refresh them well in ice water, let drain, and then mix with peanut oil and salt. Season them with red pepper flakes and crushed garlic and roast in a perforated container over direct heat for 7 minutes, stirring often.

Cauliflower in particular can also be sliced and grilled. You will find our recipe for cauliflower cutlets with a porcini mushroom rub on page 69.

Green beans

Clean the beans and blanch for 5 minutes in salted water. Refresh in ice water, let drain, and mix with olive oil, coarse sea salt and a few tablespoons of panko bread crumbs.

Put them in a preheated cast-iron frying pan over indirect heat, close the lid and cook for 10 to 15 minutes, until crispy. Don't forget to turn them over from time to time.

COOKING IN ADVANCE

Although it is possible to cook even whole hard vegetables on the grill, as you will see with our recipe for a stuffed and roasted head of cabbage on page 123, it is of course faster if potatoes and the like are cooked in advance. For some vegetables this is simply a measure to shorten the time needed to cook in the barbecue. However, cooking some vegetable varieties in advance helps them absorb the seasonings and marinades better and keeps them juicy.

Potatoes and sweet potatoes

Of course, highly popular foil-wrapped potatoes baked in the barbecue taste wonderful even without being cooked in advance. Our recipe for Hasselback potatoes with an herbed sour cream accompaniment on page 107 is a modern take on this favorite. Sweet potatoes, as seen in our recipe for stuffed sweet potatoes on page 125, can also be cooked from raw in the barbecue. If cut into not-too-thick slices, they also make delicious cutlets.

However, it is faster to make crispy potato and sweet potato halves on the barbecue if they are first parboiled and seasoned, and then grilled until golden brown.

This simply involves taking medium new potatoes or sweet potatoes, boiling them for 15 minutes in abundant water and leaving them to cool. Next, halve the unpeeled tubers and rub them with plenty of oil, coarse sea salt, a little nutmeg and some maple syrup. Place them cut side down over the grill and cook directly for 4 to 5 minutes. When the potatoes are golden, move them over to the indirect heat and roast for up to 20 minutes. New potatoes can be eaten with their skin, but sweet potatoes should be peeled.

Celeriac

It is hard to understand why celeriac is seldom cooked in a barbecue. It is prepared as deliciously juicy slices

in our recipe for barbecued celeriac steak with fennel rub on page 85.

The cooked celeriac also absorbs the aromas from the marinade very well. Marinate the still-hot slices in a mixture of olive oil, plenty of garlic, and sumac overnight in the refrigerator. Grill the slices briefly over high heat and serve very hot.

Carrots

Carrots have their place at a cookout, and not just in the salad! Whole carrots that are cooked in advance also absorb the aromas from marinades very well and become quite sweet and juicy. Coat still-hot and very wet carrots in a spicy seasoning made from tarragon, thyme, chili powder and sea salt, and grill over direct heat for a few minutes. They make an excellent garnish for barbecued tofu, which is dealt with in the next section.

THE RIGHT WAY TO BARBECUE TOFU

"I hate the taste of tofu, even when it isn't barbecued," "I simply don't like the texture of tofu" or simply "Tofu always burns on the barbecue." We often hear these and other similar arguments. Our reply is typically, "You've just never tried really good tofu." And this is true in most cases.

RULE #1: BUY GOOD QUALITY TOFU

There is tofu and there is *tofu*. By this we do not only mean the difference between soft silken tofu, which is not suitable for barbecuing, and firm tofu. As far as texture is concerned, there is a big difference between them. But also with regard to flavor. Essentially, tofu is not made from standard soybeans, and each tofu maker has their own particular recipe, which gives the final product its own distinct flavor.

For barbecuing, it is better to use firm but moist and elastic tofu that does not crumble.

RULE #2: PRESS TOFU

Tofu contains a lot of liquid, which means that it can be stored without drying out, but this also makes it difficult to put flavor into it.

You can very easily press it to remove the excess water. There are special tofu presses available, which makes sense if you eat a lot of tofu and eat it often. However, you can also just use two plates, paper towels and a heavy pot. Line a plate with paper towels and put the tofu block on it. Cover with more paper towels and with the second plate. Weigh the whole thing down with a pot or other heavy object. Take off the weight after about 20 minutes and the tofu is ready for the next step.

RULE #3: FREEZE TOFU

Here's an insider's tip from Japan that you have to try: Whole, well-drained tofu blocks are completely frozen, and then left to thaw on a plate lined with paper towels. The excess liquid is released during thawing and the tofu becomes firmer and more absorbent. It is quite normal for tofu to turn yellow when frozen.

RULE #4: SLICE TOFU PROPERLY

You should not cut tofu into thin slices. The soft bean curd can barely offer any resistance to hard barbecue tongs, so turning thin tofu slices over will be more exciting than a James Bond film. You cannot go wrong if you cut the tofu into slices about 1¼ inches (3 cm) thick.

RULE #5: MARINATE WELL FOR A LONG TIME

As previously explained, tofu has a naturally mild flavor, so it can be enhanced by means of a strongly flavored marinade and spices.

Cut the pressed or thawed tofu into thick slices and immerse them in a large amount of marinade for several hours. Seasoning mixtures containing olive oil, coarse sea salt, paprika and ground cumin work quite well.

Our recipe for London-style peppered tofu steak on page 63 is quite fiery.

RULE #6: USE PLENTY OF OIL

Dry tofu will stick to a grill faster than you can count to three. To prevent this, tofu slices seasoned with a dry rub should be brushed with plenty of oil before being placed on the grill, and any marinades should contain a large proportion of oil. Brushing the grill with oil before laying the tofu over it will ensure that the tofu will reach your plate whole.

RULE #7: SEAR OVER DIRECT HEAT; FINISH COOKING OVER INDIRECT HEAT

Tofu is particularly suited to the newest cast-iron grills, because they are good for leaving char marks and you can create the patterns you like on it. Sear the tofu slices over direct heat for about 3 minutes each side, and leave them over indirect heat for 6 to 8 more minutes to become crispy.

THE RIGHT WAY TO BARBECUE TEMPEH

Unlike tofu, tempeh is a soy product that lends itself easily to barbecuing. If you bear these few tips in mind, nothing can go wrong.

RULE #1: BLANCH TEMPEH

Cut the tempeh into slices and blanch for 7 to 10 minutes in salted water. Then drain and pat them dry. Blanched tempeh becomes flexible, loses its pungent smell and taste, and absorbs marinades better.

RULE #2: MARINATE WELL

Unlike tofu, tempeh has a very characteristic flavor, which is why mild and light marinades made with such ingredients as garlic, lemon juice, mustard, sea salt and olive oil work wonderfully.

For the same reason, tempeh only needs to be marinated for a short time—30 minutes should be enough, although it can be left longer if you have more time.

RULE #3: SKEWER

Of course, grilled tempeh slices taste fantastic, as you will see in our recipe for BBQ tempeh sandwiches on page 53.

Marinated tempeh is also good cut into large cubes and skewered with different vegetables, such as yellow and red bell peppers, blanched broccoli, and red onions.

THE RIGHT WAY TO BARBECUE SEITAN

If your neighbor loudly voices his scorn for marinated zucchini strips every time he comes over for dinner, you can pacify him with a really good seitan steak. Throw a few more on the barbecue because we can promise you that everybody else at the table will at least want to "try" one.

RULE #1: SEASON THE SEITAN AS YOU MAKE IT

You have the opportunity to add seasoning to the seitan preparation as you make it. Mix herbs and spices directly into the vital wheat gluten. Soy sauce, tomato paste and other condiments can be stirred in with the liquid to make the dough.

RULE #2: MARINATE WELL

Regardless of Rule #1, seitan can also be marinated. It will taste even better and more intense if left for at least 30 minutes or even overnight in a strongly flavored marinade.

RULE #3: USE PLENTY OF OIL

Since the way we prepare seitan uses very little fat, you will need to give your seitan steak a little help. Either add a few tablespoons of oil to the marinade or brush the seitan and the grill with extra oil before cooking.

RULE #4: BASTE OFTEN AS YOU COOK

If you follow our seitan recipes, we can assure you that when you leave the seitan skewers on the grill for a bit longer, they will stay moist. However, to make sure no hard crust forms, we recommend that you brush regularly with the leftover marinade.

RULE #5: SEAR OVER DIRECT HEAT; FINISH COOKING OVER INDIRECT HEAT

Just like tofu, seitan works really well when seared over high heat. After it develops pretty char marks, place it over indirect heat and leave it there to finish cooking. And just to remind you: don't forget to baste!

BURGERS, SANDWICHES & PATTIES

QUINOA AND CHICKPEA BURGERS

WITH BURGER SAUCE

MAKES 4 BURGERS	BARBECUING TIME 10 MINUTES	PREPARATION TIME 30 MINUTES

FOR THE PATTIES

$\frac{1}{2}$ cup (100 g) quinoa

1 tablespoon chia seeds

1 red onion

4 tablespoons olive oil

4 cremini mushrooms

$\frac{1}{2}$ teaspoon salt

$1\frac{1}{2}$ cups (250 g) cooked chickpeas

1 tablespoon soy sauce

1 tablespoon apple cider vinegar

1 tablespoon maple syrup

$\frac{1}{2}$ cup (40 g) rolled oats

2 garlic cloves, minced

$\frac{1}{2}$ teaspoon ground allspice

$\frac{1}{2}$ teaspoon ground cinnamon

FOR THE BURGER SAUCE

1 shallot

3 tablespoons finely chopped bread and
butter pickles (page 195)

$\frac{1}{4}$ cup (55 g) vegan yogurt (see tip page 183)

2 tablespoons ketchup

2 teaspoons agave nectar

1 pinch salt

EXTRAS

4 sweet potato buns (see page 207)

4 handfuls salad greens

$\frac{3}{4}$ cup (60 g) finely chopped red cabbage

How about a scrumptious burger with a crispy grilled quinoa patty, delicious burger sauce and fresh salad greens? Yes, please!

1. Prepare the quinoa according to the instructions on the package. Then let cool.

2. Grind the chia seeds, mix with $\frac{1}{4}$ cup (60 ml) water and set aside.

3. Thinly slice the onion. Put 1 tablespoon of the olive oil into a hot frying pan and fry the onion over medium heat for 7 minutes. Dice the mushrooms and gently stir into the onion. Season with $\frac{1}{4}$ teaspoon salt and cook for another 5 minutes on low heat.

4. Coarsely chop the chickpeas in a food processor with the soy sauce, vinegar and maple syrup.

5. Finely grind the oats in a blender and transfer to a large mixing bowl. Add the garlic, quinoa, chia seed mixture, fried onions, chickpea paste and spices and knead well by hand. Season with $\frac{1}{4}$ teaspoon salt. Rest for 10 minutes, knead again and shape the mixture into four patties.

6. For the sauce, finely chop the shallot and mix with the other ingredients.

7. Brush the patties with the remaining 3 tablespoons olive oil and cook over direct heat for 4 to 5 minutes each side.

8. Cut the burger buns open and warm them on their cut side over direct heat for 1 minute. Cover the bottom half with salad greens, one patty and some cabbage. Top with sauce and cover with the other half of the bun.

PORTOBELLO MUSHROOM PANINI

WITH HERB PESTO

MAKES 4 PANINI	BARBECUING TIME 15 MINUTES	PREPARATION TIME 20 MINUTES

FOR THE HERB PESTO

1⅓ cups (200 g) peas (fresh or frozen)

1 handful fresh basil

1 cup (240 ml) olive oil

2 garlic cloves

2 tablespoons chopped cashews

1 tablespoon salt

FOR THE PICKLED ONIONS

2 red onions

½ cup (100 ml) apple cider vinegar

2 teaspoons agave nectar

FOR THE MUSHROOMS

8 portobello mushrooms

¼ cup (60 ml) olive oil

½ teaspoon coarse sea salt

EXTRAS

4 sourdough rye rolls

The panini will become quite flat and crispy if you weigh them down with bricks preheated over direct heat. These will add strong heat from above.

1. For the herb pesto, purée all the ingredients in a blender.

2. For the pickled onions, cut the onions into wedges, combine them with the vinegar and agave nectar in a cast-iron saucepan and bring to a boil over direct heat. Then gently braise them over indirect heat until the vinegar completely evaporates.

3. Clean the mushrooms and cut off the stems (do not throw them away; simply grill them separately and add them to the panini). Brush each cap with 1½ teaspoons olive oil, season with coarse sea salt and grill them over direct heat for 5 minutes each side.

4. Cut the bread rolls open, spread the bottom half with pesto and top with the mushrooms and pickled onions. Cover with the tops of the rolls and weigh down the panini with the preheated bricks. Grill over direct heat until crispy, 5 to 7 minutes.

TIP
The pickled onions can also be prepared ahead of time on the stove in the kitchen. In this case, cook the ingredients first over high heat and then braise them over low heat.

PLANTAIN PATTIES

WITH SMOKED TOFU

MAKES 4 PATTIES	BARBECUING TIME 10 MINUTES	PREPARATION TIME 25 MINUTES

FOR THE PATTIES

2 small yellow plantains
(13 ounces/375 g)

3 ounces (90 g) smoked tofu

½ spring onion (green and white parts)

3 garlic cloves

½ habanero pepper

¼ cup (60 ml) plus 2 tablespoons
canola oil

1½ teaspoons salt

1 teaspoon curry powder

EXTRAS

1 carrot

Juice of 1 lime

2 tablespoons olive oil

¼ teaspoon salt

1 head endive

¼ cup (55 g) vegan yogurt (see tip page 183)

¼ cup (15 g) chopped fresh parsley

In all sincerity, plantains do not receive the attention they deserve. So, are you one of those people who steer clear of them? Then you are sure to change your mind with these plantain patties, because they taste nothing like bananas.

1. Peel the plantains, cut them into large pieces and bring them to a boil in plenty of water. Cook for 5 minutes over medium heat, then drain and let cool for 10 minutes.

2. Finely dice the tofu. Finely chop the spring onion, garlic and habanero. Combine with the plantain, ¼ cup (60 ml) of the canola oil, salt and curry powder in a food processor and purée.

3. Wet your hands and shape the mixture into four patties. Brush the patties with the remaining 2 tablespoons canola oil and cook over direct heat for 4 to 5 minutes each side.

4. Grate the carrot and mix it with the lime juice, olive oil and salt. Fill the endive leaves with the mixture and top with vegan yogurt and parsley. Serve with the plantain patties.

TIP

Green plantains can be left to ripen on the counter until they are dark, nearly black even. Pack them in a paper bag and put them in a warm place until they are ripe enough.

EGGPLANT GYROS

WITH TAHINI & YOGURT SAUCE

MAKES 4 GYROS	BARBECUING TIME 10 MINUTES	PREPARATION TIME 20 MINUTES + 2 HOURS

2 small eggplants (14 ounces/400 g)

3 teaspoons coarse sea salt

1 tablespoon paprika

$\frac{3}{4}$ teaspoon dried oregano

$\frac{1}{2}$ teaspoon garlic powder

$\frac{1}{2}$ teaspoon nigella seeds

$\frac{1}{2}$ teaspoon mustard seeds

$\frac{1}{4}$ cup plus 2 tablespoons (90 ml) olive oil

1 large pita bread

1 tomato

$\frac{1}{4}$ cucumber

1 red onion

$1\frac{3}{4}$ cups (120 g) finely sliced red cabbage

8 tablespoons tahini and yogurt sauce (page 183)

4 tablespoons finely chopped fresh dill

1. Cut the eggplants into slices 1 cm thick. Mix them with $1\frac{1}{2}$ teaspoons of the salt and let sit for 10 minutes. Wash the slices under running water, drain well and pat dry.

2. Combine the remaining $1\frac{1}{2}$ teaspoons salt with the paprika, oregano, garlic powder, nigella seeds, mustard seeds and oil and stir into a marinade.

3. Add the eggplant slices to the marinade and leave for at least 2 hours. Next, grill the slices over direct heat for 3 to 4 minutes each side, take them off the grill and mix with the leftover marinade.

4. Cut the bread into quarters. Toast them over direct heat for 2 minutes.

5. Slice the tomato and cucumber. Thinly slice the onion.

6. Fill the pita quarters with eggplant slices, tomato, cucumber, onion and cabbage and top with tahini and yogurt sauce and fresh dill.

TIP
Our eggplant seasoning also works really well with tofu or seitan strips.

MEGA BEAN BURGERS

WITH GRILLED PEAR

MAKES 4 BURGERS	BARBECUING TIME 10 MINUTES	PREPARATION TIME 1 HOUR + 30 MINUTES

FOR THE PATTIES

$\frac{1}{3}$ cup (70 g) brown rice

2 tablespoons wild rice

$\frac{1}{2}$ red onion

11 tablespoons olive oil

$\frac{3}{4}$ cup (75 g) shelled walnuts

3 tablespoons sunflower seeds

2 tablespoons flaxseeds

1 teaspoon dried thyme

1 teaspoon ground cumin

1 teaspoon ground turmeric

1 teaspoon salt

$\frac{1}{2}$ teaspoon red pepper flakes

1$\frac{1}{4}$ cups (200 g) cooked black beans

3 tablespoons dried bread crumbs

EXTRAS

1 pear

4 sweet potato buns (see page 207)

4 teaspoons prepared mustard

1 handful arugula

1 shallot, finely chopped

4 teaspoons vegan mayonnaise

1. Bring the rice to a boil in $\frac{3}{4}$ cup (175 ml) water, cover and steam over low heat for 40 minutes. Let cool for 15 minutes.

2. Finely chop the onion. Put 3 tablespoons of the oil into a hot frying pan and fry the onion over medium heat for 15 minutes.

3. Combine the walnuts, sunflower seeds and flaxseeds with the herbs and spices in a food processor or mortar and grind to a fine powder.

4. Mix the rice, onion, 4 tablespoons of the oil, nut and seed mixture, beans and bread crumbs and knead by hand until smooth. Leave the mixture to rest in the refrigerator for 30 minutes.

5. Shape the mixture into four patties, brush each with 1 tablespoon of the oil and cook over direct heat for 4 to 5 minutes each side until they turn brown with grill marks and are heated through. Halve the pear and grill the halves on their cut sides for 4 minutes over direct heat, and then slice.

6. Cut the burger buns open and warm them on their cut sides on the grill for 1 minute. Cover each of the bottom halves with 1 teaspoon mustard, arugula, one burger patty, finely chopped shallot and pear slices. Top with mayonnaise and cover with the top halves of the buns.

TIP

The burgers cook quite well on a cast-iron griddle, flipped with a very thin spatula.

GRILLED ONIGIRI
WITH JAPANESE-STYLE BBQ GLAZE

MAKES 4 ONIGIRI	BARBECUING TIME 8 MINUTES	PREPARATION TIME 30 MINUTES

$\frac{3}{4}$ cup (150 g) sushi rice

1 tablespoon rice vinegar

1 teaspoon agave nectar

$\frac{3}{4}$ teaspoon salt

1 tablespoon black sesame seeds

$\frac{1}{4}$ sheet nori seaweed

1 tablespoon finely chopped fresh parsley

4 tablespoons Japanese-style
barbecue sauce (page 173)

Today we're making Japan's favorite snack food on the grill. The crispy rice balls taste especially good when paired with a fresh salad.

1. Prepare the rice according to the instructions on the package. Let cool and season with the vinegar, agave nectar and salt.

2. Toast the sesame seeds in a dry frying pan over medium-low heat until fragrant. Take care not to burn them.

3. Finely chop the seaweed and parsley. Carefully mix the seaweed, parsley and sesame seeds into the rice.

4. Wet your hands and shape the seasoned rice into four balls. Use you fingers at an angle to mold the rice into large triangles and press well.

5. Brush each onigiri with 1 tablespoon Japanese-style barbecue sauce and grill over direct heat for 3 to 4 minutes, until crispy.

TIP
Onigiri are great when filled. Diced avocado and finely grated carrots make delicious fillings.

GRILLED VEGGIE SUBS

MAKING GRILLED VEGETABLES COOL

MAKES 4 SANDWICHES	BARBECUING TIME 25 MINUTES	PREPARATION TIME 35 MINUTES + 20 MINUTES

1 eggplant

1 zucchini

1 tablespoon plus 2 teaspoons
coarse sea salt

1 yellow bell pepper

4 tablespoons olive oil

1 garlic clove

2 tablespoons chopped fresh parsley

3 tablespoons apple cider vinegar

4 ciabatta rolls

2 handfuls arugula

Is barbecuing zucchini slices too boring for you? We understand completely. But you can bring them to life by combining them with eggplant and peppers in a crispy sandwich.

1. Cut the eggplant and zucchini lengthwise into slices 1 cm thick. Mix the slices with 1 tablespoon plus 1 teaspoon of the salt and lay them over paper towels. Let sit for 30 minutes, then rinse the slices under running water and wipe them dry.

2. Quarter the pepper and lay the pieces on their skin side over direct heat without oil for 5 to 6 minutes, until they turn black. Take them off the grill, cover them with a damp cloth, leave for 2 minutes to steam and then peel them.

3. Mix the vegetables with 2 tablespoons of the oil. Cook them over indirect heat for 15 to 20 minutes with the lid closed, brushing with the remaining 2 tablespoons oil and turning them over from time to time.

4. For the marinade, mince the garlic and mix with the remaining 1 teaspoon salt, parsley and vinegar. Remove the vegetables from the barbecue and soak them in the marinade for 20 minutes.

5. Cut the ciabatta rolls open and warm them on their cut sides over direct heat for 2 minutes. Fill them with the vegetables and top with arugula.

TIP

In the unlikely event that there are any leftovers, the grilled and marinated vegetables can keep for up to 14 days in the refrigerator in an airtight container.

BBQ TEMPEH SANDWICHES

WITH STEWED FIG & ONION MARMALADE & ARUGULA

MAKES 4 SANDWICHES	BARBECUING TIME 10 MINUTES	PREPARATION TIME 45 MINUTES

FOR THE MARMALADE

1¼ cups (180 g) dried figs

4 red onions

2 tablespoons olive oil

½ teaspoon ground cinnamon

½ teaspoon salt

1 bay leaf

½ cup (100 ml) red wine vinegar

FOR THE TEMPEH

One 8-ounce (225 g) package tempeh

¼ cup plus 2 tablespoons (90 ml) soy sauce

¼ cup plus 1 tablespoon (75 ml) olive oil

1 teaspoon smoked paprika

EXTRAS

4 sandwich rolls

4 tablespoons vegan cream cheese

2 handfuls arugula

1. For the marmalade, dice the figs and slice the onions into thin rings. Put the olive oil in a hot cast-iron saucepan and add the figs, onions, cinnamon, salt and bay leaf and sweat them for 5 minutes over indirect heat. Deglaze the pan with the vinegar and ⅔ cup (150 ml) water and cook over low heat for 40 minutes.

2. Cut the tempeh into slices 1 cm thick, blanch for 10 minutes in boiling water, then drain.

3. Mix the soy sauce, oil and paprika and marinate the tempeh slices in the mixture for 30 minutes.

4. Cook the tempeh over direct heat for 4 to 5 minutes each side.

5. Cut the rolls open and spread each cut side with 1 tablespoon vegan cream cheese. Fill each with the arugula and tempeh and top with 1 to 2 tablespoons of the fig and onion marmalade.

TIP
The marmalade is also very good if prepared beforehand and can be stored for up to 1 week in the refrigerator.

PULLED MUSHROOM SANDWICHES

WITH CRISPY OYSTER MUSHROOMS

MAKES 4 SANDWICHES	BARBECUING TIME 15 MINUTES	PREPARATION TIME 5 MINUTES + 30 MINUTES

2 tablespoons olive oil

¼ cup plus 2 tablespoons (90 ml) basic barbecue sauce (page 173)

11 ounces (300 g) oyster mushrooms

1 large carrot

4 sweet potato buns (see page 207)

4 tablespoons vegan mayonnaise

2 handfuls baby spinach

1. Mix the oil with the barbecue sauce. Mix the mushrooms with the marinade and let sit for 30 minutes.

2. Cook the mushrooms over direct heat for 4 to 5 minutes each side. Then put them over indirect heat and leave for another 7 minutes to turn crispy. Next, take them off the grill and tear them into strips.

3. Thinly slice or grate the carrot.

4. Cut the burger buns open and toast them on their cut side over direct heat for 2 minutes. Spread each bottom half with 1 tablespoon mayonnaise and top with baby spinach, mushrooms and carrot. Cover with the top half of the buns.

TIP
You can also tear the mushrooms into strips before marinating and cook them on a hot cast-iron griddle or in a cast-iron frying pan.

TOFU SANDWICHES

WITH MARINATED FENNEL

MAKES 4 SANDWICHES	**BARBECUING TIME** 10 MINUTES	**PREPARATION TIME** 10 MINUTES + 2 HOURS

FOR THE TOFU

1 pound (500 g) tofu

2 garlic cloves

1 tablespoon chopped fennel fronds

$2\frac{1}{2}$ teaspoons fennel seeds

1 teaspoon coarse sea salt

$\frac{1}{2}$ teaspoon black pepper

3 tablespoons olive oil

1 tablespoon agave nectar

FOR THE MARINATED FENNEL

2 small fennel bulbs

1 teaspoon coarse sea salt

2 tablespoons lemon juice

FOR THE REMOULADE

$\frac{1}{4}$ cup plus 2 tablespoons (85 g) vegan yogurt
(see tip page 183)

$\frac{1}{4}$ cup (55 g) vegan mayonnaise

2 tablespoons chopped fennel fronds

2 tablespoons chopped fresh chives

2 tablespoons chopped fresh parsley

$\frac{1}{2}$ teaspoon salt

4 sandwich rolls

1 tablespoon chopped fennel fronds

1. Cut the tofu into slices 1.5 cm thick. Crush the garlic, fennel fronds and seeds, salt, pepper, oil and agave nectar to a paste in a mortar. Coat the tofu with the paste and let marinate in the refrigerator for 2 hours.

2. For the marinated fennel, thinly slice the fennel bulbs, mix them with the salt and lemon juice and rub the slices well with your hands.

3. Mix the remoulade ingredients well.

4. Take the tofu out of the marinade and drain briefly. Cook over direct heat for 4 to 5 minutes, brushing with the leftover marinade from time to time.

5. Cut the rolls open and warm them on their cut sides over direct heat for 2 minutes. Fill them with remoulade, tofu slices and marinated fennel and top with chopped fennel fronds.

TIP
The marinated fennel can be prepared beforehand and left overnight in the refrigerator.

GRILLED CHEESE SANDWICHES

WITH VEGAN MOZZARELLA

MAKES 4 SANDWICHES	BARBECUING TIME 15 MINUTES	PREPARATION TIME 15 MINUTES

2 shallots

4 tablespoons olive oil

4 ounces (120 g) button mushrooms

7 ounces (200 g) spinach

4 garlic cloves

8 cherry tomatoes

4 balls vegan mozzarella (page 199)

8 thick slices sandwich bread

4 tablespoons bread and butter pickles
(page 195)

Grilled cheese sounds so unvegan. But they are also fabulous after grilling, and that way they guarantee you a challenge, right?

1. Finely dice the shallots. Put 2 tablespoons of the oil in a cast-iron frying pan and sweat the shallots for 2 minutes over indirect heat. Slice the mushrooms and add them to the shallots. Leave for another 2 minutes to soften.

2. Coarsely chop the spinach, mince the garlic and halve the tomatoes. Add them all to the pan and cook for 3 to 5 minutes, stirring often.

3. Slice the mozzarella. Brush four slices of bread with the remaining 2 tablespoons olive oil and cover each with the spinach mixture, mozzarella slices and 1 tablespoon pickles, then top with the remaining slices of bread.

4. Grill the sandwiches over direct heat for 3 minutes each side, then place them over indirect heat for 8 minutes for the cheese to melt.

TIP
You can cook the spinach mixture in the kitchen beforehand so it will only take a short time to prepare the sandwiches before grilling.

STEAKS, SAUSAGES & SKEWERS

PEPPERED TOFU STEAKS

LONDON STYLE

MAKES 4 STEAKS	**BARBECUING TIME** 15 MINUTES	**PREPARATION TIME** 10 MINUTES + 4 HOURS

2 garlic cloves

¼ cup (60 ml) olive oil

2 tablespoons soy sauce

2 tablespoons vegan Worcestershire sauce

2 tablespoons balsamic vinegar

1 tablespoon agave nectar

2 teaspoons freshly ground black pepper

1 teaspoon freshly ground pink pepper

1 teaspoon fresh rosemary

14 ounces (400 g) frozen and thawed tofu
(see page 31)

Unseasoned tofu never draws people over to the barbecue—that's a fact. However, nobody can resist our delicious, peppery marinated tofu steaks—that's a promise.

1. For the marinade, mince the garlic and mix with the remaining ingredients, except the tofu, until smooth.

2. Cut the tofu into slices 2 cm thick, add them to the marinade and leave for 4 hours in the refrigerator.

3. Oil the grill and sear the tofu steaks over direct heat for 3 to 4 minutes each side, then finish cooking them over indirect heat with the lid closed for another 3 minutes each side. Baste often with the leftover marinade.

TIP
You can achieve attractive char marks if you sear the steaks on a cast-iron grill. It is best to use a particularly thin stainless steel spatula to turn them over.

GRILLED BRATWURST

OR "2 IN A ROLL"

MAKES 8 SAUSAGES	BARBECUING TIME 10 MINUTES	PREPARATION TIME 45 MINUTES

$1\frac{1}{4}$ cups (140 g) vital wheat gluten

1 tablespoon cornstarch

1 tablespoon nutritional yeast

2 teaspoons salt

$1\frac{1}{2}$ teaspoons onion powder

$\frac{1}{2}$ teaspoon ground ginger

$\frac{1}{2}$ teaspoon ground nutmeg

$\frac{1}{2}$ teaspoon black pepper

1 pinch ground allspice

1 garlic clove, minced

1 tablespoon vegetable oil

1 tablespoon agave nectar

EXTRAS

$\frac{1}{4}$ cup (60 ml) canola oil

4 white hot dog buns

8 teaspoons prepared mustard

With both of us being natives of Germany, it is a matter of honor for us to throw a few vegan bratwurst sausages on the barbecue.

1. Mix together the dry ingredients, then mix in the wet ingredients with $1\frac{1}{4}$ cups (300 ml) lukewarm water, first stirring with a wooden spoon and then kneading well by hand.

2. Cut the dough into eight portions. Shape each piece by hand into a sausage and roll each one tightly in an 8 x 8-inch (20 x 20 cm) sheet of plastic wrap. Knot the ends.

3. Put the sausages in a steamer and steam them for 30 minutes. Let cool completely. Remove the plastic wrap.

4. Brush the sausages with the canola oil and grill them over direct heat for 3 to 4 minutes each side.

5. Warm the buns in the barbecue for 2 minutes, cut them open, fill each with two sausages and top with mustard.

TIP
Our bratwurst can be prepared in advance and even frozen so you will always have a supply for your next barbecue.

GRILLED KING OYSTER MUSHROOMS

IN BALSAMIC VINEGAR & THYME MARINADE

MAKES 4 SKEWERS	BARBECUING TIME 16 MINUTES	PREPARATION TIME 5 MINUTES + 30 MINUTES

9 ounces (250 g) king oyster mushrooms

3 garlic cloves

$\frac{1}{4}$ cup (60 ml) balsamic vinegar

$\frac{1}{4}$ cup (60 ml) olive oil

1 tablespoon fresh thyme

$\frac{1}{2}$ teaspoon salt

Deliciously marinated, juicy mushrooms cooked on the barbecue are an amazing explosion of flavor. Our grilled king oyster mushrooms in a balsamic vinegar and thyme marinade are not to be missed.

1. Clean the mushrooms and halve them lengthwise.

2. For the marinade, mince the garlic and mix with the remaining ingredients until smooth.

3. Add the mushrooms to the marinade, stir well and leave for at least 30 minutes in the refrigerator.

4. Thread the mushrooms onto bamboo skewers that have been soaked in water. Cook over indirect heat for 8 minutes each side.

CAULIFLOWER CUTLETS

WITH PORCINI MUSHROOM RUB

MAKES 4 CUTLETS	BARBECUING TIME 30 MINUTES	PREPARATION TIME 25 MINUTES

$\frac{1}{2}$ cup (20 g) dried porcini mushrooms

2 teaspoons black pepper

1 teaspoon salt

2 garlic cloves

$\frac{1}{4}$ cup (60 ml) plus 2 tablespoons olive oil

$\frac{3}{4}$ teaspoon grated lemon zest

1 large head cauliflower

1. For the rub, finely grind the mushrooms, pepper and salt, mince the garlic and mix together with $\frac{1}{4}$ cup (60 ml) plus 1 tablespoon of the oil and the lemon zest until smooth. Rest for 15 minutes.

2. Cut four slices $1\frac{1}{4}$ inches (3 cm) thick from the cauliflower and coat them all completely with the rub.

3. Brush the cutlets with the remaining 1 tablespoon oil and cook over direct heat for 5 minutes each side. Then put them over indirect heat, close the lid and finish cooking for 15 to 20 minutes.

TIP
You can use the leftover cauliflower to make fried "rice" or as the filling for our portobello mushrooms with a creamy spinach Alfredo sauce filling (page 109).

TANDOORI TOFU SKEWERS

WITH MINT, CUCUMBER & YOGURT SAUCE

MAKES 4 SKEWERS	BARBECUING TIME 20 MINUTES	PREPARATION TIME 5 MINUTES + 4 HOURS

FOR THE SKEWERS

$\frac{1}{4}$ cup (55 g) vegan yogurt (see tip page 183)

1 large red chile pepper, stemmed
(seeded for less heat)

1 garlic clove

1 teaspoon ground coriander

1 teaspoon ground turmeric

1 teaspoon ground cinnamon

1 teaspoon salt

1 star anise

$1\frac{1}{2}$ tablespoons tomato paste

1 tablespoon peanut oil

14 ounces (400 g) tofu

EXTRAS

4 grilled chapatis (see page 211)

8 tablespoons mint, cucumber
and yogurt sauce (page 183)

1 lemon, cut into wedges

Now it's time for Indian-style barbecuing. Our succulent tofu skewers in a spicy marinade will convert even the biggest tofu skeptics.

1. For the skewers, blend the yogurt with the remaining ingredients, except the tofu, in a food processor or blender.

2. Cut the tofu into $1\frac{1}{2}$-inch (4 cm) cubes and add them to the marinade. Marinate for at least 4 hours in the refrigerator.

3. Thread the cubes onto metal skewers and cook over indirect heat with the lid closed for 10 minutes. Turn the skewers over and cook for another 8 minutes. Baste with the leftover marinade.

4. Serve the skewers with the chapatis, mint, cucumber and yogurt sauce and lemon wedges.

TIP
These skewers cook better if a skewer rack is used. This way the tofu does not come into contact with the grill and cannot stick.

VEGAN SPARERIBS

WITH A DELICIOUS BBQ GLAZE

MAKES 14 RIBS	BARBECUING TIME 15 MINUTES	PREPARATION TIME 50 MINUTES

1⅔ cups (200 g) vital wheat gluten

2 tablespoons nutritional yeast

1 tablespoon cornstarch

2 teaspoons garlic powder

1 teaspoon paprika

1 teaspoon ground fennel seed

¾ cup (175 ml) pineapple juice

½ apple, grated

½ red onion, grated

2 tablespoons soy sauce

3 tablespoons olive oil

1 teaspoon prepared mustard

EXTRAS

¾ cup (180 ml) basic barbecue sauce (page 173)

2 tablespoons olive oil

Our succulent vegan spareribs are sure to turn heads at your next barbecue.

1. Preheat the oven to 350°F (180°C).

2. Mix the vital wheat gluten, nutritional yeast, cornstarch, garlic powder, paprika, fennel seed, pineapple juice, apple, onion, soy sauce, and 2 tablespoons of the olive oil. Stir first with a wooden spoon and then knead well by hand.

3. Spread the dough over a 9 x 13-inch (23 x 33 cm) baking sheet lined with parchment paper and press firmly with the back of your hand. Cut vertically down the middle and then make six cuts across the dough.

4. Mix the remaining 1 tablespoon olive oil and mustard until smooth. Brush evenly over the seitan and bake for 35 minutes. Then let cool.

5. Mix the barbecue sauce with the oil and brush evenly over the spareribs.

6. Sear the brushed side for 4 minutes over direct heat, then turn the ribs over and finish cooking them over indirect heat with the lid closed for 10 minutes.

TIP
Our vegan spareribs can be kept warm for some time over indirect heat. They make good-size portions, don't they?

SPANISH-STYLE TAPAS SKEWERS

WITH MOJO SAUCE

MAKES 4 SKEWERS	BARBECUING TIME 20 MINUTES	PREPARATION TIME 25 MINUTES

8 medium potatoes

Coarse sea salt (see tip)

12 Padrón or shishito peppers

¼ cup (60 ml) olive oil

1 lemon

½ cup (120 ml) gazpacho-mojo (page 179)

1. Put the potatoes in a pot with plenty of water and the salt and bring to a boil. Boil for 15 minutes over medium heat, then turn off the heat and drain the water. Return the pot to the still-hot burner, cover with a lid and let the potatoes steam for 5 minutes, shaking the pot often.

2. Halve the potatoes and thread them onto bamboo skewers that have been soaked in water, alternating each potato half with a pepper. Brush the skewers with oil and sear them over direct heat for 2 to 3 minutes each side, then finish cooking them over indirect heat for another 7 minutes each side.

3. Cut the lemon into wedges and caramelize them over direct heat for 3 to 4 minutes each side.

4. Serve the skewers with the gazpacho-mojo and lemon wedges.

TIP
To make Spanish-style "wrinkled potatoes," add as much salt as needed so that a single potato added to the water will be unable to sink to the bottom of the pot (about ¼ cup/75 g per quart/liter).

EGGPLANT STEAKS

WITH MISO GLAZE

MAKES 4 STEAKS	BARBECUING TIME 30 MINUTES	PREPARATION TIME 5 MINUTES + 30 MINUTES

FOR THE STEAKS

2 eggplants

8 tablespoons peanut oil

FOR THE MISO GLAZE

$\frac{1}{4}$ cup plus 2 tablespoons (90 ml) rice wine

2 tablespoons miso paste

2 tablespoons maple syrup

EXTRAS

2 spring onions

2 teaspoons red pepper flakes

1. Halve the eggplants and coat each cut side with 1 tablespoon of the oil. Let sit for 30 minutes.

2. Grill the eggplants on their cut sides over direct heat for 5 minutes. Then turn them over, brush them with the remaining 4 tablespoons oil and cook for 10 minutes over indirect heat with the lid closed.

3. Mix together all the ingredients for the glaze.

4. Brush the eggplants with the glaze and cook for another 10 to 15 minutes over indirect heat with the lid closed.

5. Finely chop the spring onions and sprinkle them over the eggplants together with the red pepper flakes.

TIP

If you set up your barbecue with the Death Star arrangement (see page 21), you can add some water to the container on the charcoal grate and steam the eggplants at the same time. This will cut the cooking time by 4 to 5 minutes.

SEITAN STEAKS

WITH LEMON & MAPLE SYRUP GLAZE

MAKES 4 STEAKS	BARBECUING TIME 15 MINUTES	PREPARATION TIME 1 HOUR + 4 HOURS

FOR THE STEAKS

1¼ cups (150 g) vital wheat gluten

2 tablespoons nutritional yeast

1 tablespoon cornstarch

1½ teaspoons salt

1 teaspoon black pepper

1 teaspoon paprika

¼ beet, roughly chopped

2 tablespoons white vinegar

1 tablespoon prepared mustard

1 tablespoon neutral vegetable oil

FOR THE MARINADE

¼ cup (60 ml) olive oil

2 tablespoons maple syrup

2 teaspoons grated lemon zest

EXTRAS

4 tablespoons flavored butter (page 177)

A classic at any vegan barbecue, our super juicy seitan steaks with their lemon and maple syrup glaze go very well with our grilled asparagus (page 115).

1. For the steaks, mix together the vital wheat gluten, nutritional yeast, cornstarch, salt, pepper and paprika. Blend the beet together with ⅔ cup (160 ml) water and the vinegar, mustard and oil. Combine the two mixtures and knead by hand into a smooth dough.

2. Roll out the dough thinly and fold it over a few times. Repeat the operation 2 or 3 times while pressing down firmly with the back of your hand. The more you press, the better the consistency.

3. Shape the dough into a large loaf and cut it into four steaks. Put the steaks in a steamer and steam for 45 minutes.

4. For the marinade, mix together the ingredients until smooth.

5. Add the hot steaks to the marinade and marinate for at least 4 hours, preferably overnight.

6. Grill the steaks over direct heat for 5 to 7 minutes each side, brushing from time to time with the leftover marinade. Serve with the butter.

TIP
You can achieve attractive char marks if you sear the steaks on a cast-iron grill. In this case, the cooking time is reduced to 4 to 6 minutes per side.

BBQ ONION SKEWERS

WITH POMEGRANATE GLAZE

MAKES 4 SKEWERS	BARBECUING TIME 20 MINUTES	PREPARATION TIME 10 MINUTES + 4 HOURS

FOR THE MARINADE

Juice of 2 oranges

$\frac{1}{4}$ cup plus 2 tablespoons (110 g) pomegranate molasses

$\frac{1}{4}$ cup plus 2 tablespoons (90 ml) olive oil

2 teaspoons pink peppercorns

$\frac{1}{2}$ teaspoon salt

FOR THE SKEWERS

4 large onions

EXTRAS

Pomegranate tabbouleh (page 159)

White bean hummus (page 181)

1. Combine all the ingredients for the marinade in a saucepan and bring to a boil. Cook over low heat for 5 minutes.

2. Cut the onions into slices 1 cm thick and thread them onto metal skewers.

3. Pour the boiling marinade over the skewers and leave for at least 4 hours in the refrigerator.

4. Sear the onion skewers over direct heat for 4 to 5 minutes each side, then finish cooking them over indirect heat with the lid closed for another 8 to 10 minutes. Baste often with the leftover marinade.

5. Serve with the pomegranate tabbouleh and the hummus.

TIP

Mild-flavored Spanish onions are particularly suitable for our BBQ onion skewers. Red onions also taste wonderful grilled.

EGGPLANT HOT DOGS

WITH BREAD & BUTTER PICKLES

MAKES 4 HOT DOGS	BARBECUING TIME 20 MINUTES	PREPARATION TIME 10 MINUTES + 8 HOURS

FOR THE EGGPLANT HOT DOGS

4 slender Japanese eggplants

$\frac{1}{4}$ cup plus 2 tablespoons (90 ml) olive oil

1$\frac{1}{2}$ teaspoons salt

1 teaspoon ground fennel seed

$\frac{1}{2}$ teaspoon dried oregano

$\frac{1}{2}$ teaspoon garlic powder

$\frac{1}{2}$ teaspoon paprika

$\frac{1}{4}$ teaspoon dried marjoram

EXTRAS

2 tomatoes

2 shallots

4 hot dog buns

4 tablespoons bread and butter pickles
(page 195)

4 teaspoons prepared mustard

Do something different with eggplants; for instance, turn them into sausages. Sausages? Yes, sausages!

1. Peel the eggplants and combine them with the other ingredients in a food-storage bag. Seal the bag and marinate the eggplants overnight in the refrigerator.

2. Sear the eggplants over direct heat for 4 to 5 minutes each side, then finish cooking them over indirect heat with the lid closed for another 10 minutes.

3. Dice the tomatoes and cut the shallots into thin rings.

4. Cut open the buns and warm them over indirect heat for 2 minutes.

5. Fill each bun with one eggplant, tomato, shallot and pickles and top with mustard.

TIP
Instead of the slender Japanese eggplants, you can also use a large eggplant, quartered lengthwise.

CELERIAC STEAKS

WITH FENNEL BBQ RUB

MAKES 4 STEAKS	BARBECUING TIME 10 MINUTES	PREPARATION TIME 20 MINUTES + 4 HOURS

FOR THE STEAKS

1 celeriac, peeled and trimmed

¼ cup (60 ml) olive oil

¼ cup (60 ml) apple cider vinegar

3 tablespoons soy sauce

2 tablespoons maple syrup

FOR THE RUB

1 tablespoon plus ½ teaspoon fennel seeds

1½ teaspoons coriander seeds

1 teaspoon coarse sea salt

1 teaspoon black pepper

½ teaspoon fresh rosemary

Who would have thought celeriac had hidden talents? For instance, it works wonderfully as hearty and juicy steaks.

1. Cut the celeriac into slices 1 inch (2.5 cm) thick. Put the slices in a saucepan with plenty of water and bring to a boil. Parboil for 15 minutes over medium heat.

2. Mix the oil, vinegar, soy sauce and maple syrup until smooth. Add the still-hot celeriac slices and marinate for at least 4 hours in the refrigerator.

3. For the rub, crush all the ingredients in a mortar.

4. Take the celeriac out of the marinade and dredge the slices in the rub, turning them over and pressing well.

5. Grill the steaks over direct heat for 4 to 5 minutes each side.

BRUSSELS SPROUT SKEWERS

WITH DATES, GARLIC & LEMON SLICES

MAKES 4 SKEWERS	BARBECUING TIME 18 MINUTES	PREPARATION TIME 15 MINUTES + 30 MINUTES

FOR THE SKEWERS

5 ounces (150 g) brussels sprouts

1 lemon

8 garlic cloves (unpeeled)

12 pitted dates

FOR THE MARINADE

2 tablespoons olive oil

½ teaspoon toasted sesame oil

½ teaspoon coarse sea salt

EXTRAS

4 handfuls salad greens

4 tablespoons tahini and yogurt sauce
(page 183)

2 tablespoons sesame seeds

1. Blanch the brussels sprouts in plenty of salted water for 5 minutes. Then refresh in cold water.

2. Thinly slice the lemon. Thread the brussels sprouts, unpeeled garlic cloves, dates and lemon slices onto bamboo skewers that have been soaked in water.

3. For the marinade, mix together the ingredients until smooth.

4. Add the skewers to the marinade and leave for at least 30 minutes in the refrigerator.

5. Sear the skewers over direct heat for 3 to 4 minutes each side, then finish cooking them over indirect heat with the lid closed for another 10 minutes. Brush the skewers with the leftover marinade from time to time.

6. Serve with salad greens and the tahini and yogurt sauce sprinkled with sesame seeds.

TIP
Try our brussels sprout skewers also with dried apricots or fresh pineapple pieces.

SPICY CHORIZO

SMOKY, TANGY & EXTRA DELICIOUS

MAKES 8 SAUSAGES	BARBECUING TIME 10 MINUTES	PREPARATION TIME 45 MINUTES

2½ cups (300 g) vital wheat gluten

2 tablespoons nutritional yeast

1 tablespoon cornstarch

1 tablespoon hot smoked paprika

2½ teaspoons fennel seeds

2 teaspoons garlic powder

3 tablespoons cooked basmati rice

3 tablespoons soy sauce

2 tablespoons olive oil, plus 2 tablespoons for grilling

1 tablespoon tomato paste

Yes, it sounds a bit like we're showing off, but in all seriousness, this chorizo is award winning. And you wouldn't want to miss out on an award-winning vegan chorizo, would you?

1. Mix the dry ingredients, then separately mix the wet ingredients with 2 cups (500 ml) water. Next, mix them together, first stirring with a wooden spoon and then kneading well by hand.

2. Cut the dough into eight portions. Shape each piece by hand into a sausage and roll each one tightly in an 8 x 8-inch (20 x 20 cm) sheet of plastic wrap. Knot the ends.

3. Put the sausages in a steamer and steam for 30 minutes. Let cool completely. Remove the plastic wrap.

4. Brush the sausages with olive oil and grill them over direct heat for 4 to 5 minutes each side.

TIP
Spanish Padrón peppers make quite a good accompaniment for our chorizo. Brush the peppers with a little olive oil and roast them in a cast-iron frying pan or on a griddle. Serve them with coarse sea salt.

VEGETABLES STUFFED, GRILLED & BRAISED

ZUCCHINI PARCELS
WITH SEASONED SPELT FILLING

MAKES 4 PARCELS	BARBECUING TIME 8 MINUTES	PREPARATION TIME 20 MINUTES + 25 MINUTES

$\frac{2}{3}$ cup (125 g) spelt berries

1 cup (250 ml) vegetable broth

$\frac{1}{2}$ yellow onion

2 garlic cloves

1 tablespoon olive oil,
plus 2 tablespoons for grilling

1 tablespoon white wine

1 tablespoon soy sauce

1 tablespoon agave nectar

1 teaspoon fresh thyme

1 teaspoon ground fennel seed

1 large zucchini

1. Pulse the spelt in a food processor until most of the berries are broken but not too floury. Combine the spelt and vegetable broth, bring to a boil and cook over low heat for 12 minutes. Then cover with the lid and let sit for 10 minutes.

2. Finely chop the onion and garlic. Put the oil in a hot frying pan and sweat the onion and garlic over medium heat for 2 minutes. Add the spelt and fry for 3 minutes.

3. Deglaze the pan with the wine, soy sauce and agave nectar, season with the thyme and fennel and cook over low heat for 5 minutes.

4. Use a vegetable peeler to cut the zucchini into thin slices. Make crosses by laying 2 slices vertically and placing 2 slices horizontally over them. Add the filling and fold over the slices to form parcels. Press lightly.

5. Brush the parcels with oil and cook over direct heat for 3 to 4 minutes each side.

TIP
You can also season the spelt with a good amount of red pepper flakes and some oregano for Mexican-style zucchini parcels.

ROASTED CARROTS

WITH FRUITY LEMON OIL

MAKES 4 SIDE SERVINGS	BARBECUING TIME 8 MINUTES	PREPARATION TIME 10 MINUTES + 1 HOUR

21 ounces (600 g) small carrots with stems, peeled

3 tablespoons coconut oil

2 tablespoons lemon juice

2 teaspoons grated lemon zest

$1\frac{1}{2}$ teaspoons *baharat* spice mixture

1 teaspoon salt

$\frac{1}{2}$ cup (30 g) chopped fresh parsley

1. Blanch the carrots for 5 minutes, then drain and refresh under cold running water.

2. Melt the coconut oil and mix with the lemon juice, lemon zest, baharat and salt. Add the carrots and marinate for 1 hour in the refrigerator.

3. Cook the carrots over direct heat for 2 minutes each side. Then put them over indirect heat, close the lid and finish cooking for 4 minutes. Sprinkle with the parsley and serve.

TIP

Baharat is a Middle Eastern spice mixture. It is typically a blend of black pepper, paprika, coriander, cloves, cumin, cardamom, nutmeg and cinnamon. Alternatively, you can use your favorite curry spices.

GRILLED ARTICHOKES

WITH LEMONY GARLIC & THYME AIOLI

MAKES 4 ARTICHOKES	**BARBECUING TIME** 8 MINUTES	**PREPARATION TIME** 25 MINUTES + 20 MINUTES

4 large artichokes

Juice of 1 lemon

$\frac{1}{4}$ cup (60 ml) olive oil

$\frac{3}{4}$ teaspoon salt

FOR THE AIOLI

1 garlic clove

$\frac{1}{4}$ cup (55 g) vegan mayonnaise

$1\frac{1}{2}$ tablespoons lemon juice

1 teaspoon grated lemon zest

$\frac{1}{2}$ teaspoon fresh thyme

$\frac{1}{4}$ teaspoon salt

FOR THE PANGRATTATO

3 ounces (90 g) stale ciabatta bread

1 tablespoon olive oil

1 garlic clove

2 tablespoons chopped fresh parsley

$\frac{1}{2}$ teaspoon salt

Artichokes in Italy are cooked whole, directly over the embers. Since that takes a rather long time, we have created a shortcut version to satisfy artichoke cravings more quickly. Dusting them with this special *pangrattato* topping adds flavorful crunch and even greater satisfaction.

1. Halve the artichokes and trim off the tips of the leaves. Remove the chokes and steam the artichoke halves in a steamer for 20 minutes.

2. Mix together the lemon juice, oil and salt. Add the still-hot artichokes and marinate for at least 20 minutes.

3. For the aioli, mince the garlic and combine with the other ingredients. Mix until smooth.

4. For the pangrattato, cut the ciabatta into slices. Coat the slices with oil and toast over direct heat for 1 to 2 minutes. Combine with the other ingredients in a mortar and crush finely.

5. Sear the artichokes on their cut sides over direct heat for 3 to 4 minutes. Turn them 45 degrees and leave them on the grill for another 3 to 4 minutes to develop char marks.

6. Top the artichokes with pangrattato and serve with the aioli.

TIP

For the authentic Italian experience, fill the spaces between the artichoke leaves with the marinade. Insert the stems halfway into the embers of the coals, which should have cooled somewhat. After about $1\frac{1}{2}$ hours, remove the charred outer leaves and serve.

STUFFED GREEN PEPPERS

WITH PEARL BARLEY & GARLIC MARINARA SAUCE

MAKES 4 SERVINGS (8 HALF PEPPERS)	BARBECUING TIME 45 MINUTES	PREPARATION TIME 35 MINUTES

FOR THE PEARL BARLEY STUFFING

1 cup (200 g) pearl barley

1 teaspoon salt

½ bunch parsley

FOR THE GARLIC MARINARA SAUCE

1 onion

2 tablespoons olive oil

1 garlic clove

1½ cups (375 g) tomato *passata* or purée

1 teaspoon dried oregano

½ teaspoon salt

4 large green bell peppers

2 tablespoons olive oil

4 balls vegan mozzarella (page 199)

Pearl barley is mostly used in soups and stews, but it also makes a great stuffing.

1. For the stuffing, prepare the pearl barley with the salt according to the instructions on the package. Finely chop the parsley and gently mix into the barley.

2. For the marinara sauce, finely chop the onion. Put the oil in a hot saucepan and sweat the onion over medium heat until it turns translucent. Mince the garlic.

3. Deglaze the pan with the passata, add the garlic, oregano and salt and cook over low heat for 10 minutes.

4. Halve the peppers lengthwise and clean them. Coat the halves with oil. Fill them with the pearl barley and marinara sauce. Tear up the mozzarella balls and top the peppers with the pieces.

5. Cook the stuffed peppers over indirect heat with the lid closed for 35 to 45 minutes.

TIP

You can also stuff red or yellow bell peppers with the pearl barley and garlic marinara sauce. Hollowed and stuffed zucchini halves are also delicious.

GRILLED BOK CHOY

WITH GINGER GLAZE & PEANUTS

MAKES 4 SIDE SERVINGS	**BARBECUING TIME** 12 MINUTES	**PREPARATION TIME** 5 MINUTES + 30 MINUTES

4 small heads bok choy

$\frac{1}{4}$ cup (60 ml) light soy sauce

1 tablespoon dark soy sauce

2 tablespoons toasted sesame oil

2 teaspoons grated ginger

1$\frac{1}{2}$ teaspoons sesame seeds

$\frac{1}{2}$ teaspoon black pepper

2 tablespoons coarsely chopped peanuts

1. Halve the bok choy lengthwise.

2. Mix together the soy sauces, sesame oil, ginger, sesame seeds, and black pepper. Pour the mixture over the bok choy and marinate for at least 30 minutes in the refrigerator.

3. Grill the bok choy halves on their cut sides over direct heat for 4 minutes. Then turn them over and finish cooking them over indirect heat with the lid closed for 8 minutes.

4. Sprinkle the peanuts over the bok choy halves.

TIP

Try this recipe using halved heads of romaine lettuce in place of bok choy. You can even grill them over high heat so they turn a little crispy.

GRILLED CORN ON THE COB

WITH LIME & CILANTRO BUTTER

MAKES 4 EARS	BARBECUING TIME 20 MINUTES	PREPARATION TIME 15 MINUTES

FOR THE BUTTER

$\frac{1}{4}$ bunch cilantro

3 tablespoons (50 g) vegan butter,
at room temperature

2 teaspoons grated lime zest

1 teaspoon salt

4 ears fresh sweet corn

1 lime, cut into wedges

There is nothing better than fresh corn on the cob cooked on the barbecue with zesty, melty vegan butter. Mmm, delicious!

1. For the butter, finely chop the cilantro leaves and mix it together with the vegan butter, lime zest and salt. Refrigerate.

2. Grill the sweet corn over indirect heat for 15 to 20 minutes.

3. Serve with the lime and cilantro butter and lime wedges.

TIP
You can also use a knife to cut the kernels off the cob and enjoy them in tacos, burritos and wraps, or in a salsa.

GRILLED SPRING ONIONS

WITH ROMESCO SAUCE

MAKES 4 SIDE SERVINGS	BARBECUING TIME 18 MINUTES	PREPARATION TIME 10 MINUTES

FOR THE ROMESCO SAUCE

$\frac{1}{3}$ cup (50 g) almonds

$\frac{1}{4}$ cup (25 g) shelled walnuts

2 tablespoons pine nuts

2 small tomatoes

3 sun-dried tomatoes

$\frac{1}{2}$ red chile pepper, stemmed
(seeded for less heat)

2 garlic cloves

$\frac{1}{4}$ cup plus 1 tablespoon (75 ml) olive oil

$\frac{1}{4}$ cup (60 ml) red wine vinegar

2 tablespoons tomato paste

$\frac{1}{2}$ teaspoon salt

FOR THE SPRING ONIONS

2 bunches large spring onions

2 tablespoons olive oil

1 teaspoon coarse sea salt

Catalans sure know the right way to celebrate onion season. Once a year in a party called a *calçotada*, large spring onions are roasted over an open fire and enjoyed in a messy meal with delicious romesco sauce and one or several glasses of red wine. You can now hold your own calçotada in your own garden. What are you waiting for?

1. Process all the ingredients for the romesco sauce into a paste with $\frac{1}{2}$ cup (120 ml) water in a food processor using the pulse function.

2. Mix the spring onions with the oil and salt.

3. Grill the onions over direct heat for 15 to 18 minutes, turning them over often. Remove the charred outer layer, leaving the delicious and juicy interior. Serve with the romesco sauce.

HASSELBACK POTATOES

WITH HERBED SOUR CREAM & TOMATO CONFIT

MAKES 4 SIDE SERVINGS	BARBECUING TIME 50 MINUTES	PREPARATION TIME 20 MINUTES

FOR THE POTATOES

4 large potatoes

4 tablespoons flavored butter (page 177), chopped

FOR THE TOMATO CONFIT

7 ounces (200 g) small, fragrant tomatoes

4 garlic cloves

2 tablespoons olive oil

½ teaspoon coarse sea salt

FOR THE HERBED SOUR CREAM

½ garlic clove

⅔ cup (150 g) vegan sour cream

2 tablespoons chopped fresh chives

2 tablespoons chopped fresh parsley

½ teaspoon apple cider vinegar

½ teaspoon salt

¼ teaspoon black pepper

Get ready! These will be the best potatoes and tomatoes you've ever tasted. Are we exaggerating? Try them; we're eager to know what you think.

1. Make thin slices across the width of each potato, all along its length. Do not cut all the way through the potatoes. Tip: Put the potato between two chopsticks, with one chopstick along each side lengthwise, to hold it steady while you slice and to keep from slicing all the way through.

2. Place small pieces of the flavored butter on the potatoes, wrap them in parchment paper and hold each closed with a toothpick.

3. Cook the potatoes over indirect heat for 45 to 50 minutes.

4. For the tomato confit, combine the ingredients in a small cast-iron frying pan and cook them at the same time as the potatoes over indirect heat for 30 minutes.

5. For the herbed sour cream, mince the garlic and mix together with the other ingredients.

6. Serve the potatoes and tomatoes with the herbed sour cream.

TIP
You can prepare the sour cream in advance. It will keep in the refrigerator for 2 to 3 days.

STUFFED BABY BELLA MUSHROOMS

WITH CREAMY SPINACH ALFREDO SAUCE FILLING

MAKES 8 MUSHROOMS	BARBECUING TIME 25 MINUTES	PREPARATION TIME 20 MINUTES

FOR THE FILLING

½ large head cauliflower (14 ounces/400 g)

¾ cup (200 ml) nondairy milk

3 garlic cloves

3 tablespoons nutritional yeast

2 teaspoons salt

1 handful baby spinach

8 large baby bella mushrooms

3 tablespoons olive oil

3 balls vegan mozzarella (page 199), shredded

Smoky grilled mushrooms with a creamy spinach Alfredo sauce filling. Yes, please!

1. For the filling, cut the cauliflower into florets and cook for 10 minutes in plenty of water over medium heat.

2. Drain the cauliflower and transfer to a blender. Add the milk, garlic, nutritional yeast and salt and purée. Combine the purée with the spinach in a saucepan and bring to a boil. Cook for 5 minutes.

3. Clean the mushrooms and cut off the stems; finely chop the stems and add them to the filling. Brush the mushrooms with the oil, fill them and top with the vegan mozzarella.

4. Cook the mushrooms over indirect heat with the lid closed for 20 to 25 minutes.

GRILLED STUFFED GRAPE LEAVES

FILLED WITH DELICIOUS HERBED QUINOA

MAKES 30 GRAPE LEAVES	BARBECUING TIME 10 MINUTES	PREPARATION TIME 50 MINUTES

1 cup (150 g) quinoa

1 onion

2 garlic cloves

1 tomato

¼ bunch parsley

2 tablespoons raisins

4 tablespoons olive oil

2 teaspoons ras el hanout spice mixture

2 teaspoons salt

30 grape leaves (in brine)

1 lemon, sliced

Everybody knows and loves stuffed grape leaves from Middle Eastern delicatessens. However, when made at home, filled with quinoa and grilled, they give a delicious new meaning to "finger food"; take our word for it! They go particularly well dipped in our tahini and yogurt sauce (page 183).

1. Prepare the quinoa according to the instructions on the package.

2. Finely chop the onion, garlic, tomato and parsley, and coarsely chop the raisins.

3. Put 2 tablespoons of the oil in a hot frying pan and sweat the onion over medium heat for 5 minutes.

4. Add the garlic, tomato and raisins and cook for another 5 minutes.

5. Season with the spices and remove the pan from the heat. Stir in the parsley.

6. Put 1 to 2 tablespoons filling on each grape leaf. Fold the short sides over the filling first and then roll up the leaves tightly.

7. Brush the grape leaves with the remaining 2 tablespoons oil and cook over direct heat for 3 to 5 minutes each side. Serve with the lemon slices.

CRISPY POTATO SKINS

WITH GUACAMOLE FILLING

MAKES 12 POTATO HALVES	BARBECUING TIME 11 MINUTES	PREPARATION TIME 20 MINUTES

FOR THE POTATOES

6 medium potatoes

3 tablespoons olive oil

1 teaspoon salt

FOR THE GUACAMOLE FILLING

1 red chile pepper, stemmed
(seeded for less heat)

1 avocado

1 tablespoon plus 1 teaspoon lime juice

½ teaspoon salt

EXTRAS

3 tablespoons chopped cilantro

2 limes, cut into wedges

Crispy barbecued finger food. These are perfect as hors d'oeuvres or as a starter served with our craft beer and vegetable chili (page 127).

1. Boil the potatoes with their skins on and let cool. Halve them and scoop out the flesh, leaving 5 mm over the skin. Set aside the potato flesh.

2. For the guacamole filling, finely chop the chile. Halve, pit and peel the avocado. Mash the potato flesh and the avocado with a fork and mix in the remaining ingredients.

3. Brush the potato skins with the oil and grill them on their cut sides over high heat for 3 to 4 minutes. Turn them over, season with salt, fill with the guacamole, and finish cooking for another 3 minutes with the lid closed.

4. Top with the cilantro and serve with lime wedges.

GRILLED ASPARAGUS

WITH BLACK PEPPER DRESSING

MAKES 4 SIDE SERVINGS	BARBECUING TIME 6 MINUTES	PREPARATION TIME 5 MINUTES + 1 HOUR

2 pounds (1 kg) green asparagus

FOR THE DRESSING

3 sprigs mint

$\frac{1}{2}$ cup (60 ml) olive oil

Juice of 1 lemon

2 tablespoons coarsely ground black pepper

Grilled green asparagus is really easy to make—and tastes incredibly good with our seitan steaks (page 79).

1. Clean the asparagus spears and cut off the woody ends.

2. For the dressing, chop the mint leaves and mix with the rest of the ingredients.

3. Add the asparagus to the dressing and marinate for at least 1 hour in the refrigerator.

4. Grill the asparagus over direct heat for 4 to 6 minutes, turning them over from time to time.

TIP
The barbecued asparagus also tastes delicious with Sichuan peppercorns and drizzled with toasted sesame oil.

BRAISED RADISHES

IN BLACK PEPPER BUTTER

MAKES 4 SIDE SERVINGS	BARBECUING TIME 15 MINUTES	PREPARATION TIME 15 MINUTES

1 pound (500 g) radishes

1 teaspoon sea salt

3 tablespoons vegan butter

2 tablespoons coarsely ground black pepper

2 teaspoons grated lemon zest

1. Halve the radishes, season them with salt and let sit for 10 minutes. Then rinse in plenty of water.

2. Heat a cast-iron frying pan over direct heat. Melt the butter in the pan, add the radishes and pepper, and braise over indirect heat for 12 to 15 minutes, turning them from time to time.

3. Stir in the lemon zest shortly before they finish cooking.

TIP

If you do not have a cast-iron frying pan handy, you can also braise the radishes *en papillote*. Wrap the same ingredients in four parchment-paper parcels and cook over indirect heat for 15 to 20 minutes.

VEGETABLES—STUFFED, GRILLED & BRAISED

GRILLED AVOCADOS

WITH BEANS IN BOURBON BBQ SAUCE

MAKES 4 AVOCADO HALVES	BARBECUING TIME 9 MINUTES	PREPARATION TIME 20 MINUTES

FOR THE BEANS

1 shallot

$1\frac{1}{2}$ teaspoons canola oil

$\frac{3}{4}$ cup (150 g) cooked butter beans

$\frac{3}{4}$ cup (150 g) cooked kidney beans

$\frac{1}{4}$ cup (60 ml) basic barbecue sauce (page 173)

2 tablespoons bourbon

1 pinch smoked paprika

$\frac{1}{2}$ teaspoon salt

FOR THE AVOCADOS

2 avocados

1 tablespoon olive oil

EXTRAS

$\frac{1}{2}$ bunch cilantro

$\frac{1}{4}$ cucumber

1 lime, cut into wedges

Beans, bourbon, a smoky aroma and lightly seared avocados: the Wild West on a plate.

1. For the beans, finely dice the shallot. Put the oil in a hot saucepan and sweat the shallot over medium heat for 4 minutes, or until it turns translucent.

2. Add the remaining ingredients for the beans and cook over low heat for 10 minutes, stirring from time to time.

3. Halve the avocados and remove the pits. Brush the avocado halves on their cut sides with the olive oil and grill on their cut sides over direct heat for 4 minutes. Turn them over, fill them with the bean mixture and cook for another 5 minutes over indirect heat.

4. Chop the cilantro and dice the cucumber. Top the avocado halves with cilantro and cucumber and serve with lime wedges.

TIP
The avocados should be served piping hot, but they can also be reheated.

SMOKED ONIONS

COOKED ON A GRILLING PLANK

MAKES 4 ONIONS	BARBECUING TIME 1 HOUR	PREPARATION TIME 20 MINUTES

4 large Spanish onions

2 tablespoons chopped fresh parsley

$\frac{1}{4}$ cup (60 ml) olive oil

$\frac{1}{2}$ teaspoon salt

Onions cooked on a grilling plank open up a whole new world of flavor— and also look fantastic. Will family and friends be impressed by your new barbecuing skills? You bet!

1. Cut off the tips of the onions and make sixteen vertical cuts around the outside of the onion, from top to bottom, like longitudinal lines on a globe.

2. Place the onions in ice water for 10 minutes, then drain them and fan out the segments.

3. Mix the parsley with the oil and salt and spread it over the onions.

4. Arrange the onions on two grilling planks and place them over direct heat until they begin to smoke. Then put them over indirect heat, close the lid and cook for 50 to 60 minutes.

TIP
The grilling planks have to be soaked in plenty of water for at least 1 hour before use.

VEGETABLES—STUFFED, GRILLED & BRAISED

STUFFED CABBAGE

WITH LENTILS, MUSHROOMS & VEGETABLES

MAKES 4–8 SIDE SERVINGS	BARBECUING TIME 2 HOURS	PREPARATION TIME 10 MINUTES

1 medium cabbage

1 small onion

3 button mushrooms

⅓ cup (60 g) brown lentils

⅔ cup (150 ml) vegetable broth

2 tablespoons white wine vinegar

2 tablespoons herb and garlic butter
(page 177)

When you tell your guests that you have been braising a whole cabbage for two hours over glowing briquettes, they will all look up to you as a true pitmaster. But this recipe is actually very easy to make and takes little time to prepare; you can easily assemble the cabbage right next to the barbecue.

1. Make a circular incision around the cabbage stem and hollow out the cabbage, leaving a thickness of 2 cm (the inside will be great for coleslaw).

2. Finely chop the onion and mushrooms, combine with the lentils and fill the cabbage with the mixture. Pour in the broth and vinegar and top with the butter.

3. Put the cabbage over low, indirect heat and cook for 2 hours with the lid closed. Slow-burning briquettes are particularly suitable for this.

4. Remove any blackened outer leaves before serving.

TIP
The cabbage makes an excellent serving dish from which guests can help themselves. Cut it in such a way that each one can take some cabbage together with the filling.

STUFFED SWEET POTATOES

WITH CASHEW AIOLI & ALFALFA SPROUTS

MAKES 4 SWEET POTATOES	BARBECUING TIME 45 MINUTES	PREPARATION TIME 10 MINUTES + 8 HOURS

FOR THE CASHEW AIOLI

$1\frac{1}{2}$ cups (200 g) cashews

3 garlic cloves

2 teaspoons apple cider vinegar

1 teaspoon salt

$\frac{1}{2}$ teaspoon prepared mustard

FOR THE POTATOES

4 sweet potatoes

1 teaspoon coarse sea salt

4 tablespoons olive oil

EXTRAS

1 handful alfalfa sprouts

$\frac{1}{2}$ bunch cilantro

Everyone knows how to cook a baked potato in a barbecue. But smoky, stuffed sweet potatoes from the grill are something new.

1. Soak the cashews overnight in plenty of water. Drain and rinse them well under running water.

2. Prick the sweet potatoes all over with a fork. Coat them with salt and oil and wrap them in parchment paper. Bake the sweet potatoes in their parcels over indirect heat with the lid closed for 30 to 45 minutes.

3. For the cashew aioli, combine all the ingredients with $\frac{3}{4}$ cup (200 ml) water in a blender and purée.

4. Cut the sweet potatoes open, fill them with the aioli and sprouts and top with cilantro sprigs.

CRAFT BEER AND VEGETABLE CHILI

COOKED IN A DUTCH OVEN

MAKES 4 SERVINGS	BARBECUING TIME 1 HOUR	PREPARATION TIME 15 MINUTES

1 Spanish onion

1 red bell pepper

1 red chile pepper, stemmed
(seeded for less heat)

3 carrots

1 ear sweet corn

4 garlic cloves

3 tablespoons olive oil

1 heaping cup (200 g) cooked navy beans

1 heaping cup (200 g) cooked black beans

1 heaping cup (200 g) cooked kidney beans

1½ teaspoons salt

1 teaspoon ground cumin

1 teaspoon smoked paprika

1 teaspoon dried oregano

1 cup (250 ml) pale ale or Schwarzbier
(German dark lager)

⅔ cup (150 ml) vegetable broth

2 cups (350 g) chopped tomatoes

2 tablespoons tomato paste

2 ounces (50 g) dark chocolate, chopped

4 tablespoons vegan yogurt
(see tip page 183)

½ bunch cilantro

Our vegetable chili, with its delicious aroma of craft beer and chocolate, is not only for your summer barbecue. It can also be made on the barbecue in winter, when there can be nothing better than a warming stew. And while the chili stews, other things can be cooked over the direct heat around the Dutch oven.

1. To preheat the Dutch oven, arrange the briquettes in a ring in the barbecue. Place the Dutch oven in the middle of the grill. Close the lid of the pot and the barbecue and let preheat for 10 minutes.

2. Chop the onion, bell pepper, chile and carrots. Cut the corn kernels off the cob and mince the garlic.

3. Add the oil to the Dutch oven and sweat the onion for 3 minutes while stirring constantly. Add the bell pepper, chile, carrots, corn, garlic, beans and spices and fry for 5 minutes.

4. Deglaze the pot with the beer and broth and stir in the tomatoes, tomato paste and chocolate.

5. Cover the Dutch oven with the lid and either place five or six glowing briquettes on the lid or close the barbecue. Stew for 45 minutes. Take the lid off the Dutch oven and leave for another 15 minutes to reduce. For an even smokier flavor, add some soaked smoking chips over the embers and close the barbecue.

6. Serve with vegan yogurt and cilantro leaves.

STUFFED TOMATOES

WITH HEMP & ALMOND PESTO

MAKES 4 TOMATOES	BARBECUING TIME 20 MINUTES	PREPARATION TIME 1 HOUR

$\frac{3}{4}$ cup (160 g) brown rice

FOR THE HEMP AND ALMOND PESTO

$\frac{1}{2}$ bunch parsley

$\frac{1}{2}$ bunch basil

$\frac{1}{2}$ cup (120 ml) olive oil

$\frac{1}{4}$ cup (40 g) hulled hemp seeds

2 tablespoons chopped almonds

1 teaspoon salt

4 beefsteak tomatoes

1 ball vegan mozzarella (page 199), sliced

2 tablespoons olive oil

1. Bring the rice to a boil in 1 cup (240 ml) water and steam over low heat with the lid closed for 40 minutes.

2. For the pesto, combine all the ingredients in a blender and purée.

3. Mix the pesto with the rice.

4. Carefully scoop out the contents of the tomatoes and fill them with the pesto rice. Cover with slices of vegan mozzarella and drizzle with oil.

5. Put the tomatoes in a barbecue-safe pan or in a cast-iron frying pan over indirect heat and cook with the lid closed for 20 minutes.

TIP
If you are in a hurry, you can use any vegan pesto to make the filling for our grilled tomatoes.

PIZZA, WRAPS & Co.

PIZZA ARRABBIATA

WITH CHILE MARINARA SAUCE & FENNEL

MAKES 4 PIZZAS	BARBECUING TIME 5 MINUTES PER PIZZA	PREPARATION TIME 20 MINUTES + 1 HOUR

FOR THE PIZZA CRUST

One ¼-ounce (7 g) packet active dry yeast

4¼ cups (500 g) white spelt flour

2 teaspoons salt

FOR THE CHILE MARINARA SAUCE

2 garlic cloves

1 red chile pepper, stemmed
(seeded for less heat)

¾ cup (175 g) tomato passata or purée

⅔ cup (175 g) tomato paste

¼ cup (60 ml) olive oil

¼ cup (60 ml) agave nectar

1 tablespoon plus 1 teaspoon dried oregano

2 teaspoons salt

FOR THE FENNEL

1 fennel bulb

1 tablespoon lemon juice

½ teaspoon salt

EXTRAS

20 Kalamata olives, pitted

1 handful fresh basil

4 tablespoons coarse-ground cornmeal

1. To preheat the pizza stone, spread the contents of a full chimney starter of briquettes over the charcoal grate. Heat the pizza stone for 45 minutes. Then fill the chimney starter a few more times with charcoal and add it to the barbecue, and if possible a few sticks of firewood, and wait for another 10 minutes.

2. For the pizza crust, stir the yeast into 1⅓ cups (320 ml) warm water and set aside until the yeast has dissolved. Mix the flour and salt, and then add the liquid. Stir with a wooden spoon to obtain a smooth batter.

3. Knead the dough by hand for 10 minutes on a floured work surface. Put the dough in a bowl, cover and leave in a warm place for 1 hour, or until it has doubled in size.

4. For the marinara sauce, mince the garlic, finely dice the chile and mix with the remaining ingredients until smooth.

5. For the fennel, thinly slice the fennel bulb, mix with the lemon juice and salt and rub the slices well with your hands.

6. Divide the dough into four uniform pieces and roll each one out into a pizza crust. Spread sauce over the crusts and cover with the fennel, olives, and basil leaves. Sprinkle 1 tablespoon cornmeal over the pizza stone and lay a pizza on it. Bake on the barbecue over high heat with the lid closed. At a temperature of about 575°F (300°C), the pizza should take 4 to 5 minutes to cook; at a lower temperature, adjust the cooking time accordingly.

SHISH KEBAB WRAPS

WITH SPICY SEITAN MEDALLIONS

MAKES 4 WRAPS	BARBECUING TIME 14 MINUTES	PREPARATION TIME 50 MINUTES + 4 HOURS

FOR THE SEITAN

2 cups (225 g) vital wheat gluten

3 tablespoons nutritional yeast

1 tablespoon cornstarch

2 teaspoons paprika

1 teaspoon ground cumin

1 teaspoon garlic powder

$\frac{3}{4}$ teaspoon ground cinnamon

$\frac{1}{2}$ teaspoon black pepper

$\frac{1}{2}$ teaspoon salt

$3\frac{1}{2}$ ounces (100 g) beets

2 tablespoons soy sauce

2 tablespoons vegan Worcestershire sauce

2 tablespoons olive oil

1 tablespoon light molasses

FOR THE MARINADE

1 garlic clove

2 tablespoons apple cider vinegar

2 tablespoons olive oil

EXTRAS

$\frac{1}{2}$ each of a red, green and yellow bell pepper

1 red onion

1 tomato, chopped

$\frac{1}{2}$ cucumber, sliced

4 grilled chapatis (page 211)

4 tablespoons mint, cucumber and yogurt sauce (page 183)

1. Thoroughly mix together the vital wheat gluten, nutritional yeast, cornstarch, paprika, cumin, garlic powder, cinnamon, pepper and salt.

2. Combine the beets, soy sauce, Worcestershire sauce, oil and molasses in a blender and purée.

3. Mix the dry and wet ingredients together by stirring with a wooden spoon, then knead the resulting dough well by hand.

4. Cut the dough into sixteen portions. Press each piece flat, fold them over and cut them into evenly sized medallions.

5. Put the medallions in a steamer and steam for 30 minutes.

6. For the marinade, mince the garlic and mix with the remaining ingredients until smooth.

7. Add the seitan medallions to the marinade and marinate for at least 4 hours in the refrigerator.

8. Cut the peppers and onion into $1\frac{1}{4}$-inch (3 cm) pieces and thread them with the seitan medallions onto metal skewers.

9. Brush the skewers with the remaining marinade and grill them over direct heat for 3 to 4 minutes each side. Then place them over indirect heat and cook for another 6 minutes, turning them from time to time.

10. Serve the skewers with chopped tomato and cucumber slices over chapatis and top with mint, cucumber and yogurt sauce.

MELANZANA PIZZA BITES

PARMIGIANA STYLE

MAKES 8 PIZZA BITES	BARBECUING TIME 20 MINUTES	PREPARATION TIME 20 MINUTES

1 large eggplant

4 teaspoons sea salt

2 large beefsteak tomatoes

2 garlic cloves

4 balls vegan mozzarella (page 199)

½ bunch basil

4 tablespoons olive oil

2 teaspoons red pepper flakes

1 teaspoon dried thyme

1 tablespoon coarsely ground black pepper

Parmigiana di melanzane—a classic of Sicilian cuisine. Italian mammas might be up in arms about it, but we're going to make it on the barbecue now. Are you in?

1. Cut the eggplant into slices 2 cm thick. Mix them with 2 teaspoons of the salt and let sit for 10 minutes. Then rinse them under running water and dry them.

2. Cut the tomatoes into slices 1 cm thick, mince the garlic, slice the mozzarella, and pluck the basil leaves off the stems.

3. Brush both sides of the eggplant slices with 2 tablespoons of the olive oil and season with the remaining 2 teaspoons salt, red pepper flakes and thyme. Place 2 or 3 basil leaves and garlic over the slices and cover with a tomato slice and mozzarella.

4. Season with black pepper and drizzle the pizza bites with the remaining 2 tablespoons olive oil.

5. Cook the pizza bites over indirect heat with the lid closed for 20 minutes.

6. Top with more basil leaves and serve.

GRILLED BUTTERNUT SQUASH TACOS

WITH BLACK BEANS & CASHEW QUESO

MAKES 12 TACOS	BARBECUING TIME 16 MINUTES	PREPARATION TIME 20 MINUTES

FOR THE CASHEW QUESO

$\frac{3}{4}$ cup (180 ml) cashew sour cream (page 175)

1 red chile pepper, stemmed
(seeded for less heat)

FOR THE SQUASH

1 pound (500 g) peeled and seeded butternut
squash (about $\frac{1}{2}$ medium squash)

2 tablespoons olive oil

FOR THE BEANS

1 onion

$\frac{1}{2}$ bunch cilantro

2 tablespoons olive oil

$2\frac{1}{3}$ cups (400 g) cooked black beans

2 tablespoons basic barbecue sauce (page 173)

2 tablespoons soy sauce

Juice of 1 lime

2 teaspoons pickled jalapeño peppers

1 teaspoon ground cumin

1 teaspoons dried oregano

12 flour tortillas

1 avocado

1 lime, cut into wedges

1. For the cashew queso, process the sour cream with the chile in a blender until smooth.

2. Cut the squash into slices 2 cm thick, coat with the oil and grill over direct heat for 3 minutes each side. Then put them over indirect heat, close the lid and finish cooking for 10 minutes. Cut them into bite-size pieces.

3. For the beans, finely dice the onion, pluck off the cilantro leaves and finely chop the stems. Preheat a cast-iron saucepan over indirect heat, add the oil and sweat the onion for 2 minutes. Add the remaining ingredients, except the cilantro leaves, and cook over indirect heat with the lid closed for 10 minutes, stirring from time to time.

4. Warm the tortillas over indirect heat for 1 minute. Halve, pit, peel and dice the avocado. Fill the tacos with the bean mixture, squash pieces and avocado. Top with the cashew queso and cilantro leaves. Serve with lime wedges.

TIP

You can prepare the beans in advance and heat them up over indirect heat in a cast-iron saucepan or a stainless steel bowl.

GRILLED TARTES FLAMBÉES

WITH SQUASH & RED ONIONS

MAKES 4 TARTS	BARBECUING TIME 10 MINUTES PER TART	PREPARATION TIME 20 MINUTES + 1 HOUR

FOR THE TART CRUST

One ¼-ounce (7 g) packet active dry yeast

4¼ cups (500 g) white spelt flour

2 teaspoons salt

¼ cup (60 ml) canola oil

FOR THE SAUCE

7 ounces (200 g) smoked tofu, roughly chopped

2 garlic cloves

½ cup (100 g) vegan yogurt (see tip page 183)

¼ cup (60 ml) lemon juice

1 tablespoon nutritional yeast

2 teaspoons fresh rosemary

2 teaspoons salt

½ teaspoon red pepper flakes

FOR THE TOPPING

7 ounces (200 g) seeded red kuri (Hokkaido) squash

1 red onion

2 ounces (50 g) smoked tofu

1 teaspoon fresh rosemary

Tarte flambée **should really be cooked on an open fire or it won't taste half as good. We vary the classic recipe by using red kuri squash, making it the perfect dish for barbecuing in autumn and winter.**

1. For the tart crust, stir the yeast into 1⅓ cups (320 ml) warm water and set aside until the yeast has dissolved. Mix the flour and salt, and then add the liquids. Stir with a wooden spoon to obtain a smooth batter.

2. Knead the dough by hand for 10 minutes on a floured work surface. Put the dough in a bowl, cover and leave in a warm place for 1 hour, or until it has doubled in size.

3. Preheat the pizza stone (see the recipe for pizza arrabbiata on page 133).

4. For the sauce, combine all the ingredients in a blender and process until smooth.

5. Cut the squash into thin wedges and the onion into thin rings. Dice the tofu.

6. Divide the dough into four uniform pieces and roll them out. Spread the sauce over the tart crusts and cover with the squash, onion and tofu. Top with rosemary. Lay one tart on the pizza stone. Bake on the barbecue over high heat for 8 to 10 minutes with the lid closed.

DEEP-DISH PIZZAS

WITH CAVOLO NERO & TOMATO SAUCE

MAKES 4 PIES	BARBECUING TIME 15 MINUTES	PREPARATION TIME 20 MINUTES + 20 MINUTES

FOR THE CRUST

2 cups (250 g) white spelt flour

$\frac{1}{4}$ teaspoon salt

$2\frac{1}{2}$ tablespoons olive oil

FOR THE FILLING

$\frac{3}{4}$ cup (175 g) tomato passata or purée

$2\frac{1}{2}$ tablespoons tomato paste

1 garlic clove

2 teaspoons dried oregano

$1\frac{1}{2}$ teaspoons muscovado or
dark brown sugar

$\frac{1}{2}$ teaspoon salt

$\frac{1}{4}$ teaspoon black pepper

10 leaves cavolo nero (lacinato kale)

EXTRAS

3 tablespoons olive oil

4 balls vegan mozzarella (page 199), sliced

1. For the crust, mix the flour and salt. Mix the oil with $\frac{1}{2}$ cup (120 ml) water. Add the liquid to the flour and mix, first stirring with a wooden spoon and then kneading well by hand. Put the dough in a bowl, cover and rest in the refrigerator for 20 minutes.

2. Divide the dough into four uniform pieces and roll them out on a well-floured work surface.

3. For the filling, mix the passata and tomato paste together. Mince the garlic and add it to the tomato mixture with the oregano, sugar, salt and pepper.

4. Remove the stems from the cavolo nero and cut the leaves into thin strips. Add them to the sauce.

5. Heat four 6- or 7-inch (16 to 18 cm) cast-iron frying pans over indirect heat with the lid of the barbecue closed.

6. Put $1\frac{1}{2}$ teaspoons of the oil in each pan. Line the pans with the dough, spread with the filling, and top with mozzarella. Drizzle the remaining 1 tablespoon oil over the pies and bake over indirect heat with the lid closed for 15 minutes.

TIP
Instead of cavolo nero, you can also use other varieties of kale, bok choy or spinach.

GRILLED PESTO TART

WITH ASSORTED TOMATOES

MAKES 1 TART	BARBECUING TIME 15 MINUTES	PREPARATION TIME 20 MINUTES + 20 MINUTES

FOR THE TART CRUST

4¼ cups (500 g) white spelt flour

1 tablespoon olive oil

¼ teaspoon salt

FOR THE HERB PESTO

1 bunch parsley

4 garlic cloves

6 Kalamata olives, pitted

¼ cup plus 1 tablespoon (75 ml) olive oil

2 tablespoons pine nuts

1 tablespoon nutritional yeast

1 teaspoon salt

FOR THE TOPPING

1 pound (500 g) assorted tomatoes

1 tablespoon olive oil

1. For the tart crust, mix all the ingredients with ¼ cup (60 ml) water, stirring with a wooden spoon. Knead the dough well by hand for 10 minutes on a floured work surface. Put the dough in a bowl, cover and rest in the refrigerator for 20 minutes.

2. Preheat the pizza stone (see the recipe for pizza arrabbiata on page 133).

3. For the pesto, combine all the ingredients in a blender and process until smooth.

4. Roll the dough out on a floured work surface into a disk 2 mm thick, lay it on the preheated pizza stone and spread with the pesto.

5. Slice the tomatoes, lay them over the tart crust and drizzle well with the oil.

6. Place the pizza stone on the grill, close the lid and bake at 400°F (200°C) for 12 to 15 minutes.

TIP
In spring you can top this with fresh green asparagus, and this pesto tart goes wonderfully with pieces of black salsify or parsnip in autumn and winter.

GRILLED QUESADILLAS

WITH APRICOT FILLING

MAKES 12 PIECES	BARBECUING TIME 14 MINUTES	PREPARATION TIME 15 MINUTES

2 shallots

1 red bell pepper

8 cherry tomatoes

3 fresh apricots

1 grilled ear sweet corn (see page 103)

1 tablespoon olive oil

½ teaspoon salt

½ batch (200 g) vegan mozzarella
(see page 199)

4 flour tortillas

4 tablespoons cashew sour cream
(page 175)

¼ bunch cilantro

1 lime, cut into wedges

Do you like Mexican finger food? Then you must try our crispy grilled quesadillas with apricots, peppers and sweet corn.

1. Finely dice the shallots and pepper. Finely chop the tomatoes and apricots. Cut the corn kernels off the cob.

2. Put the oil in a hot cast-iron saucepan, add the vegetables and apricots, and sweat them for 5 minutes over indirect heat. Season with the salt.

3. Spread the vegetable and apricot filling over two of the tortillas. Tear the mozzarella into pieces and arrange them on top. Cover with the remaining tortillas.

4. Grill the quesadillas over indirect heat for 12 to 14 minutes, carefully turning them over halfway through.

5. Cut each quesadilla into six pieces, top with cashew sour cream and cilantro leaves, and serve with lime wedges.

TIP
A good accompaniment for the grilled quesadillas is our hot pickled radishes (page 209).

VIETNAMESE PIZZAS

WITH RICE PAPER, COCONUT MILK & TURMERIC

MAKES 4 PIZZAS	BARBECUING TIME 4 MINUTES	PREPARATION TIME 10 MINUTES

2 spring onions

2 carrots

½ bunch cilantro

½ bunch mint

⅔ cup (150 ml) coconut milk

1 tablespoon plus 1 teaspoon rice flour

2 teaspoons ground turmeric

2 teaspoons nutritional yeast

4 sheets rice paper

2 tablespoons melted coconut oil

This "pizza" is extremely popular in Vietnam and is often ordered at street-food stands to be eaten straight off the grill. And we totally understand why. Either in spite of or because of its simplicity, it tastes fantastic.

1. Finely chop the spring onions and finely grate the carrots. Pluck off the mint and cilantro leaves and finely chop the leaves.

2. Mix the coconut milk, rice flour, turmeric and nutritional yeast with the onions, carrots and herbs.

3. Brush the rice paper sheets on both sides with the oil and spread the topping over each one.

4. Grill the pizzas over direct heat for 3 to 4 minutes until crispy, turning them around (not over!) often to prevent the rice paper from burning.

SALADS
FROM THE GRILL
...OR OTHERWISE

PANZANELLA

WITH TOASTED CIABATTA & ASSORTED TOMATOES

MAKES 4 SERVINGS	BARBECUING TIME 6 MINUTES	PREPARATION TIME 15 MINUTES

FOR THE SALAD

5 ounces (150 g) day-old ciabatta bread

1 tablespoon olive oil

1 pound (500 g) assorted tomatoes
(e.g., beefsteak, heirloom tomatoes, cherry
tomatoes)

$\frac{1}{4}$ cup (50 g) pitted Kalamata olives

1 teaspoon capers

$\frac{1}{2}$ red onion

FOR THE DRESSING

3 tablespoons olive oil

2 tablespoons white balsamic vinegar

1 teaspoon capers

1 garlic clove

$\frac{1}{2}$ teaspoon salt

EXTRAS

$\frac{1}{2}$ bunch basil

1. Cut the bread into slices 2 cm thick, coat them with the oil and grill them over direct heat for 2 to 3 minutes each side.

2. Chop the tomatoes. Coarsely chop the olives and capers. Cut the onion into thin strips. Cut or tear the bread into bite-size pieces and put them in a large bowl with the other salad ingredients.

3. For the dressing, combine the ingredients in a blender and purée.

4. Pour the dressing over the salad and mix well.

5. Top with basil leaves.

TIP

Use excellent-quality tomatoes, olives and olive oil,
so your panzanella will taste as it should: like summer,
the sun and Italy.

KALE SALAD

WITH SMOKY PEANUT DRESSING

MAKES 4 SERVINGS	PREPARATION TIME 15 MINUTES + 30 MINUTES

FOR THE SALAD

1 medium Chioggia beet
(about 7 ounces/200 g; see tip)

6 ounces (180 g) kale

1 carrot

2 cups (150 g) shredded red cabbage

FOR THE DRESSING

3 tablespoons peanut butter

Juice of $\frac{1}{2}$ lemon

1 tablespoon olive oil

1 tablespoon apple cider vinegar

1 tablespoon soy sauce

1 teaspoon maple syrup

$\frac{1}{2}$ teaspoon smoked paprika

$\frac{1}{4}$ teaspoon black pepper

1. Thinly slice the beet and tear the kale leaves into bite-size pieces.

2. Cut the carrot into matchsticks. Blanch the vegetables for 2 minutes and refresh in ice water. Drain well.

3. For the dressing, combine the ingredients with $\frac{1}{4}$ cup plus 2 tablespoons (90 ml) water in a blender and process until smooth.

4. Pour the dressing over the salad, mix well and refrigerate for 30 minutes before serving.

TIP
Red beets are also well suited to this kale salad. Blanch the slices 2 minutes longer.

GRILLED ZUCCHINI SALAD

WITH TOASTED PINE NUTS

MAKES 4 SERVINGS	BARBECUING TIME 24 MINUTES	PREPARATION TIME 5 MINUTES + 20 MINUTES

FOR THE ZUCCHINI

4 zucchini

$\frac{1}{4}$ cup (60 ml) olive oil

$\frac{1}{2}$ teaspoon salt

FOR THE DRESSING

2 garlic cloves

2 tablespoons olive oil

2 tablespoons white balsamic vinegar

2 teaspoons prepared mustard

1 teaspoon salt

EXTRAS

3 tablespoons toasted pine nuts

Finally: grilled zucchini! But we've given it a little twist and a delicious garlicky dressing. It simply belongs at a vegan cookout.

1. Cut the zucchini lengthwise into slices 5 mm thick. Mix them with the oil and salt and marinate for 20 minutes.

2. For the dressing, combine all the ingredients in a blender and process until smooth.

3. Grill the zucchini slices over indirect heat for 10 to 12 minutes each side, then pour the dressing over them and top with the pine nuts.

TIP

The zucchini can stay a little crunchy. The main thing is to give them a nice smoky aroma and appealing char marks. This also tastes good cold.

POMEGRANATE TABBOULEH

WITH CHICKPEAS & HERBS

MAKES 4 SERVINGS	**PREPARATION TIME** 25 MINUTES

FOR THE SALAD

$1\frac{1}{4}$ cups (200 g) couscous

1 large bunch parsley

$\frac{1}{2}$ bunch mint

$\frac{1}{2}$ red onion

4 tomatoes

$\frac{1}{2}$ cucumber

$1\frac{1}{4}$ cups (200 g) cooked chickpeas

FOR THE DRESSING

$\frac{1}{4}$ cup (60 ml) cold-pressed olive oil

Juice of 1 lemon

1 teaspoon salt

EXTRAS

$\frac{1}{4}$ cup (45 g) fresh pomegranate seeds
(see tip)

1. Prepare the couscous according to the instructions on the package.

2. Finely chop the parsley, mint leaves and onion. Core and dice the tomatoes and cucumber.

3. For the dressing, mix together the ingredients until smooth.

4. Mix the couscous, herbs, onion, tomatoes, cucumber and chickpeas with the dressing, and sprinkle with the pomegranate seeds.

TIP
Collect the juice from the pomegranate as you scoop out the seeds and add it to the dressing for even more fruitiness.

MARINATED FENNEL SALAD

WITH RED LENTILS

MAKES 4 SERVINGS	PREPARATION TIME 15 MINUTES + 10 MINUTES

FOR THE LENTILS

1 cup (200 g) dried red lentils

1⅔ cups (400 ml) vegetable broth

1 teaspoon ground fennel

½ teaspoon ground cumin

1 tablespoon white balsamic vinegar

1 teaspoon lemon juice

FOR THE FENNEL

2 fennel bulbs

1 spring onion

FOR THE DRESSING

¼ cup plus 1 tablespoon (75 ml) olive oil

2 tablespoons white balsamic vinegar

2 teaspoons lemon juice

1 teaspoon salt

½ teaspoon black pepper

Our marinated fennel is wonderfully light and refreshing. The warm lentils give the crispy vegetables an extra special touch.

1. Combine the lentils with the broth in a saucepan and bring to a boil. Cook them for 10 minutes over medium heat. Add the ground fennel and cumin after 5 minutes.

2. Clean the fennel bulbs and set aside the fronds. Thinly slice the fennel and cut the spring onion into thin rings.

3. For the dressing, mix together the ingredients.

4. Pour the dressing over the fennel and spring onion and mix well.

5. Season the lentils with vinegar and lemon juice.

6. Serve the dressed fennel and spring onion on a plate. Cover it with the warm lentils and top with finely chopped fennel fronds.

TIP
This salad is also good if prepared in advance and tastes very delicious cold.

GRILLED POTATO SALAD

WITH FRESH ARUGULA

MAKES 4 SERVINGS	BARBECUING TIME 10 MINUTES	PREPARATION TIME 25 MINUTES

FOR THE POTATOES

1 pound (500 g) small multicolored potatoes

2 tablespoons olive oil

1 teaspoon coarse sea salt

FOR THE DRESSING

1 avocado, halved, pitted and peeled

¼ cup plus 2 tablespoons (90 ml) white wine vinegar

¼ cup plus 2 tablespoons (90 ml) olive oil

3 tablespoons almond milk

Juice of 1 lemon

1 tablespoon prepared mustard

1 teaspoon salt

½ teaspoon black pepper

EXTRAS

5 cups (100 g) arugula

1 spring onion

Lovely multicolored potatoes stand out in our grilled version of the potato salad, which is making a well-deserved comeback.

1. Boil the potatoes and let cool. Halve the potatoes, mix them with the oil and salt, and grill them on their cut sides over indirect heat for 8 to 10 minutes.

2. For the dressing, combine all the ingredients in a blender and process until smooth.

3. Mix the grilled potatoes with the dressing.

4. Gently mix in the arugula and cut the spring onion into thin rings. Scatter them over the salad.

QUINOA AND BEAN SALAD

WITH FLAXSEEDS & HERB VINAIGRETTE

MAKES 4 SERVINGS	PREPARATION TIME 25 MINUTES + 30 MINUTES

FOR THE SALAD

$\frac{2}{3}$ cup (100 g) quinoa

$1\frac{2}{3}$ cups (250 g) cooked butter beans

1 cup (150 g) cooked kidney beans

1 cup (150 g) cooked black beans

2 tablespoons flaxseeds

FOR THE HERB VINAIGRETTE

$\frac{1}{2}$ bunch chives

$\frac{1}{2}$ bunch parsley

3 tablespoons olive oil

2 tablespoons apple cider vinegar

$1\frac{1}{2}$ teaspoons salt

1 teaspoon prepared mustard

1 teaspoon maple syrup

Crunchy flaxseeds, nutty quinoa and delicious beans for a protein boost. Superfoods for a cookout!

1. Prepare the quinoa according to the instructions on the package and let cool.

2. For the vinaigrette, finely chop the chives and parsley. Set aside 2 tablespoons of each for garnish. Blend all the ingredients for the vinaigrette until smooth.

3. Mix the vinaigrette into the quinoa, beans and flaxseeds. Sprinkle the salad with the reserved chives and parsley.

4. Refrigerate for 30 minutes before serving.

TIP

This salad also works well with brown rice instead of quinoa. Simply steam the rice for 40 minutes in $1\frac{1}{2}$ times its volume in water and let it cool completely.

CRUNCHY COLESLAW

WITH FRESH CHIVES & SOUR CREAM DRESSING

MAKES 4 SERVINGS	**PREPARATION TIME** 15 MINUTES + 15 MINUTES

FOR THE SALAD

$2\frac{1}{2}$ cups (175 g) shredded red cabbage

$2\frac{1}{2}$ cups (175 g) shredded green cabbage

2 teaspoons salt

1 carrot

1 tablespoon chopped fresh chives

FOR THE DRESSING

1 garlic clove

$\frac{1}{4}$ cup (60 ml) cashew sour cream (page 175)

$\frac{1}{4}$ cup (60 ml) olive oil

1 tablespoon white wine vinegar

1 tablespoon poppy seeds

This is a lot healthier than that ready-made coleslaw you get at the supermarket. And more delicious in any case.

1. Mix the cabbage with the salt and rub it in well. Let it sit for 15 minutes, then put the cabbage in a sieve and rinse under running water.

2. Finely grate the carrot and gently mix it into the cabbage with the chopped chives.

3. For the dressing, mince the garlic and mix with the remaining ingredients until smooth.

4. Pour the dressing over the salad and mix well.

TIP
The poppy seeds give the salad a distinctive touch. If you have none on hand, you can also use flaxseeds.

SICHUAN CUCUMBER SALAD

WITH GARLIC & CILANTRO

MAKES 4 SERVINGS	**PREPARATION TIME** 10 MINUTES + 10 MINUTES

2 cucumbers

2 teaspoons salt

8 garlic cloves

3 red chile peppers, stemmed
(seeded for less heat)

$\frac{1}{4}$ cup (60 ml) peanut oil

$\frac{1}{4}$ cup (60 ml) soy sauce

1 teaspoon ground Sichuan pepper

2 tablespoons cilantro leaves

Not only does our Sichuan cucumber salad taste delicious, you can also let off steam while you make it. You heard right, you can get brutal with it.

1. Use the flat side of a large kitchen knife to smash the cucumbers. You will feel much better afterward.

2. Coarsely chop up the cucumbers and mix with the salt. Let sit for 10 minutes.

3. Drain the excess liquid and wash the cucumber pieces under running water.

4. Mince the garlic and chiles. Put the peanut oil in a hot frying pan and sweat the garlic and chiles over medium heat for 2 to 3 minutes.

5. Deglaze the pan with the soy sauce and add the Sichuan pepper.

6. Pour the hot dressing over the cucumber pieces, let cool a little and sprinkle cilantro leaves over the top.

TIP
So as not to mess up the kitchen too much, put the cucumbers in a freezer bag and seal it before smashing them. Then you can reuse the bag to marinate vegetables, seitan or tofu.

SAUCES & BASICS

TRIO OF BBQ SAUCES

BASIC, JAPANESE & MEXICAN

BASIC BARBECUE SAUCE

1 onion

2 tablespoons canola oil

2 garlic cloves

2 cups (500 g) tomato passata or purée

$\frac{1}{2}$ cup (120 ml) apple cider vinegar

2 tablespoons vegan Worcestershire sauce

2 tablespoons light molasses

2 tablespoons muscovado or dark brown sugar

1 teaspoon salt

1 teaspoon paprika

1 teaspoon black pepper

$\frac{1}{2}$ teaspoon ground cinnamon

$\frac{1}{2}$ teaspoon ground star anise

$\frac{1}{4}$ teaspoon red pepper flakes

1. Finely chop the onion and combine with the oil in a hot saucepan. Sweat the onion for 5 minutes over medium heat until it turns translucent.

2. Mince the garlic, add it to the onion and cook for another 2 minutes.

3. Add the other ingredients and bring to a boil. Reduce the sauce over low heat, uncovered, for 40 minutes, stirring from time to time.

JAPANESE-STYLE BARBECUE SAUCE

$\frac{3}{4}$ cup (175 ml) basic barbecue sauce

$2\frac{1}{2}$ tablespoons dark soy sauce

$2\frac{1}{2}$ tablespoons rice vinegar

2 tablespoons light soy sauce

$1\frac{1}{2}$ teaspoons toasted sesame oil

For the Japanese-style sauce, combine all the ingredients in a blender and purée.

MEXICAN-STYLE BARBECUE SAUCE

$\frac{3}{4}$ cup (175 ml) basic barbecue sauce

3 tablespoons lime juice

2 tablespoons tequila

1 red chile pepper, stemmed (seeded for less heat)

2 teaspoons grated lime zest

$\frac{1}{2}$ teaspoon ground cumin

$\frac{1}{2}$ teaspoon dried oregano

For the Mexican-style sauce, combine all the ingredients in a blender and purée.

CASHEW SOUR CREAM

CREAMY & LIGHT

MAKES ABOUT 1 CUP (250 ML)	**PREPARATION TIME** 5 MINUTES + 8 HOURS

1 cup (125 g) cashews

¼ cup (60 ml) lemon juice

1 teaspoon nutritional yeast

½ teaspoon salt

1. Soak the cashews overnight in plenty of water.

2. Drain and rinse the cashews well under running water.

3. Combine them with the other ingredients and ⅓ cup (80 ml) water in a blender and process until smooth.

TIP
You can also make the sour cream with almonds. Extra nutty and delicious.

TRIO OF FLAVORED BUTTERS

TOMATO, HERB & SESAME

MAKES ABOUT ⅔ CUP (150 G) OF EACH	**PREPARATION TIME** 10–15 MINUTES FOR EACH

TOMATO AND CAPER BUTTER

4 sun-dried tomatoes

2 teaspoons capers

½ cup (120 g) vegan butter,
at room temperature

1 tablespoon coarsely ground black pepper

½ teaspoon salt

1. Pour boiling water over the tomatoes and let them soak for 10 minutes. Pour off the water and let them drain. Finely chop the tomatoes and capers and mix with the rest of the ingredients.

2. Transfer the soft butter to a sheet of wax paper, carefully roll it up and let harden in the refrigerator.

HERB AND GARLIC BUTTER

½ garlic clove

1 tablespoon chopped fresh chives

1 tablespoon chopped fresh parsley

1 tablespoon chopped fresh dill

½ cup (120 g) vegan butter,
at room temperature

1 tablespoon olive oil

½ teaspoon grated lemon zest

½ teaspoon salt

1. Mince the garlic and mix together with the other ingredients.

2. Transfer the soft butter to a sheet of wax paper, carefully roll it up and let harden in the refrigerator.

SESAME AND CHILE BUTTER

1 tablespoon black sesame seeds

1 tablespoon white sesame seeds

1 yellow chile pepper, stemmed
(seeded for less heat)

½ cup (120 g) vegan butter,
at room temperature

½ teaspoon salt

1. Toast the sesame seeds in a dry frying pan over medium heat until they give off a toasted fragrance. Take care not to burn them.

2. Finely chop the chile and mix together with the other ingredients.

3. Transfer the soft butter to a sheet of wax paper, carefully roll it up and let harden in the refrigerator.

GAZPACHO-MOJO

SO FRESH, SO EASY

MAKES ABOUT 1 CUP (250 ML)	**PREPARATION TIME** 5 MINUTES

2 tomatoes

½ red bell pepper

½ cucumber

2 garlic cloves

2 dried apricots

¼ cup (25 g) dried bread crumbs

3 tablespoons white wine vinegar

1 tablespoon chopped almonds

1 teaspoon salt

½ teaspoon black pepper

Is the temperature outside breaking summer heat records? Hey, we aren't ones to complain that it's 105°F (40°C) in the shade with the heat radiating from the barbecue, seeing as it's cold enough the rest of the year. However, if you fancy cooling down, try our refreshing gazpacho-mojo.

Combine all the ingredients in a blender and process until smooth.

TIP

Our gazpacho-mojo is a natural accompaniment for our Spanish-style tapas skewers (page 75), but also wonderful with grilled asparagus (page 115) and as a dip for the pull-apart bread (page 197).

WHITE BEAN HUMMUS
WITH GRILLED SHALLOTS

MAKES ABOUT 1 CUP (250 G)	BARBECUING TIME 12 MINUTES	PREPARATION TIME 5 MINUTES

2 shallots

$2\frac{1}{2}$ tablespoons olive oil

$1\frac{1}{3}$ cups (200 g) cooked butter beans

1 garlic clove

1 pitted date

Juice of $\frac{1}{2}$ lemon

1 tablespoon tahini

$\frac{1}{2}$ teaspoon salt

Everybody loves hummus, at least that's what we believe. But if you're after something new, try making our white bean hummus with grilled shallots.

1. Halve the shallots, coat them with $1\frac{1}{2}$ teaspoons of the oil and grill them on their cut sides over direct heat for 2 minutes. Then finish cooking them over indirect heat for 10 minutes, turning them over from time to time.

2. Combine the grilled shallots with the remaining 2 tablespoons oil, 2 tablespoons water and the remaining ingredients in a blender and process until smooth.

TRIO OF YOGURT SAUCES

AVOCADO, TAHINI & MINT

AVOCADO AND CILANTRO YOGURT

1 avocado, halved, pitted and peeled

$\frac{1}{2}$ bunch cilantro

$\frac{3}{4}$ cup (180 g) vegan yogurt

$1\frac{1}{2}$ tablespoons lime juice

$\frac{1}{2}$ teaspoon salt

Combine all the ingredients in a blender and process until smooth.

TAHINI AND YOGURT

1 cup (200 g) vegan yogurt

3 tablespoons tahini

$1\frac{1}{2}$ tablespoons lemon juice

1 tablespoon cold-pressed olive oil

$\frac{1}{2}$ teaspoon salt

Mix all the ingredients together.

MINT, CUCUMBER AND YOGURT

$\frac{1}{4}$ cucumber

$1\frac{1}{2}$ tablespoons chopped fresh mint

$1\frac{1}{2}$ tablespoons chopped fresh dill

$\frac{3}{4}$ cup (175 g) vegan yogurt

$\frac{1}{2}$ teaspoon salt

1. Core and dice the cucumber.

2. Mix all the ingredients together.

TIP

Although there are many vegan yogurt options available, we recommend using unsweetened soy yogurt for the recipes in this book.

GREEN CHILE SAUCE

CAUTION! HOT!

MAKES ABOUT 1 CUP (250 ML)	BARBECUING TIME 15 MINUTES	PREPARATION TIME 5 MINUTES

4 ounces (120 g) green chile peppers

1 tablespoon olive oil

4 garlic cloves

$\frac{1}{4}$ cup (60 ml) lime juice

1 teaspoon salt

Fruity, smoky and with a delicious bite, our green chile sauce goes wonderfully with steaks and sausages and makes a great spicy dip for grilled finger food.

1. Coat the chiles with $1\frac{1}{2}$ teaspoons of the oil and grill over direct heat for 5 minutes, turning them over from time to time. Then cook them over indirect heat for 8 to 10 minutes, until soft. Remove any blackened parts, although you can use the parts that have turned dark golden.

2. Cut the chiles in half and remove the stems (as well as the seeds for less heat). Combine the chile halves with the other ingredients and 3 tablespoons water in a blender and process until smooth.

SAUCES & BASICS

MANGO AND HABANERO SAUCE

CAUTION! EVEN HOTTER!

MAKES ABOUT 1 CUP (250 ML)	PREPARATION TIME 30 MINUTES

3 habanero peppers, stemmed (and seeded for less heat)

$\frac{1}{2}$ mango, peeled and pitted

3 tablespoons white vinegar

1 garlic clove

$2\frac{1}{2}$ tablespoons muscovado or dark brown sugar

$1\frac{1}{2}$ teaspoons maple syrup

1 teaspoon salt

This sauce gives a new meaning to "hot" sauce. It will heat things up nicely for you and your guests. Warning: ¡*Muy picante!*

1. Combine the habaneros with the mango, vinegar and garlic in a blender and process until smooth.

2. Boil the sugar with 2 tablespoons water and add the habanero and mango purée. Simmer, uncovered, for 20 minutes.

3. Season with the maple syrup and salt.

TIP
Our mango and habanero sauce will keep for up to 4 weeks in an airtight container in the refrigerator.

TRIO OF SALSAS

MANGO, PINEAPPLE & TOMATO

MAKES ABOUT 1 CUP (250 ML) OF EACH	**BARBECUING TIME** 15 MINUTES FOR EACH	**PREPARATION TIME** 5 MINUTES FOR EACH

MILD MANGO SALSA

1 mango

½ green bell pepper

1 tablespoon coarsely chopped cilantro

2 tablespoons fresh orange juice

1 tablespoon white wine vinegar

1 tablespoon soy sauce

1 teaspoon ground pink pepper

1 pinch salt, or more to taste

1. Peel, pit and finely dice the mango. Finely dice the pepper.

2. Mix them with the other ingredients and season with more salt if desired.

GRILLED PINEAPPLE SALSA

½ ripe pineapple

4 cherry tomatoes

½ red chile pepper, stemmed (seeded for less heat)

2 tablespoons coconut flakes

Juice of 1 lime

½ teasoon salt

1. Peel, core and slice the pineapple. Grill over indirect heat for 15 minutes, turning the slices over from time to time. Then dice them.

2. Quarter the tomatoes, slice the chile into thin rings and mix them with the other ingredients.

GRILLED TOMATO SALSA

3 tomatoes

1 jalapeño pepper

½ onion

1½ teaspoons olive oil

2 garlic cloves

2 tablespoons lime juice

2 tablespoons coarsely chopped cilantro

1 teaspoon agave nectar

1 teaspoon salt

1. Lightly prick the tomatoes with a fork. Brush the tomatoes, jalapeño and onion with the oil.

2. Grill the vegetables over indirect heat for 15 minutes, turning them over from time to time.

3. Combine all the ingredients in a food processor and coarsely chop them.

BREAD & MORE

GRANARY BREAD

BAKED IN A DUTCH OVEN

MAKES 1 LOAF	BARBECUING TIME 1 HOUR	PREPARATION TIME 20 MINUTES + 12 HOURS

1 tablespoon active dry yeast

1 teaspoon raw cane sugar

6⅔ cups (800 g) whole-grain spelt flour

¾ cup (100 g) sunflower seeds

⅔ cup (100 g) flaxseeds

⅓ cup (50 g) pumpkin seeds

1½ teaspoons salt

Nothing beats home-baked bread. The best thing about it is you can even bake it in the barbecue, and the fire gives it a really delicious smokiness.

1. Stir the yeast and sugar into 3 cups (700 ml) warm water and set aside until the yeast has dissolved.

2. Mix together the flour, sunflower seeds, flaxseeds, pumpkin seeds and salt.

3. Add the liquid to the dry ingredients and mix well. Do not knead! Cover the dough and let it rise for 12 hours.

4. To preheat the Dutch oven, arrange the briquettes in a ring in the barbecue. Place the Dutch oven in the middle of the grill. Close the lid of the pot and the barbecue and let preheat for 10 minutes.

5. Put the dough on a well-floured work surface, lightly press to flatten and fold all the sides into the middle. Line the Dutch oven with parchment paper and place the dough inside with the seam (where the sides join) on the underside.

6. Cover the Dutch oven with the lid and either place five or six glowing briquettes on the lid or close the barbecue. Bake for 45 minutes. Take the lid off the Dutch oven and leave for another 15 minutes to form a crispy crust.

7. Let cool completely.

BREAD AND BUTTER PICKLES

A MUST AT ANY BARBECUE

MAKES ABOUT 1 POUND (500 G)	**PREPARATION TIME** 20 MINUTES + 2 HOURS

$\frac{1}{2}$ cup (120 ml) apple cider vinegar

$\frac{1}{4}$ cup (50 g) raw cane sugar

1 tablespoon mustard seeds

1 teaspoon coriander seeds

1 teaspoon coarse sea salt

$\frac{1}{2}$ teaspoon red pepper flakes

1 large cucumber

Did you know that the basic idea for making pickles as a way of preserving food originally came from India? We are very thankful for this invention, and we prefer to make them ourselves in every way imaginable, because it is so easy and a lot of fun.

1. Combine all the ingredients except the cucumber in a saucepan and bring to a boil.

2. Cut the cucumber into slices 1 cm thick and add them to the pickling liquid. Bring the liquid back to a boil and leave on medium heat for 5 minutes.

3. Fill a clean, sterilized canning jar with the hot pickles and close tightly.

4. Refrigerate for at least 2 hours.

TIP
These pickles will keep for one or two months in the fridge. Unopened, they can last much longer at room temperature if properly canned (processed in a hot water bath).

PULL-APART BREAD

WITH GARLIC & ONION FILLING

MAKES 1 LOAF	BARBECUING TIME 20 MINUTES	PREPARATION TIME 10 MINUTES

4 button mushrooms

1 spring onion

¼ bunch parsley

1 loaf bread (about 1 pound/455 g white, ciabatta, spelt or other artisanal bread)

¼ cup (50 g) herb and garlic butter (page 177), coarsely chopped

Deliciously warm and soft bread from the barbecue with the aroma of herbs. Place it in the middle of the table so your guests can simply tear a piece off.

1. Finely chop the mushrooms, spring onion and parsley.

2. Make crisscross cuts across the loaf without slicing all the way through. Fill the loaf with the mushrooms, spring onion, parsley and herb butter.

3. Place the loaf over indirect heat with the lid closed for 20 minutes. Serve hot.

TIP

You can also fill the loaf with other favorite ingredients, such as sun-dried tomatoes, olives, vegan mozzarella (page 199) and basil.

VEGAN MOZZARELLA

TO MELT ON PIZZAS & SANDWICHES

MAKES ABOUT 1 POUND (500 G)	PREPARATION TIME 20 MINUTES + 32 HOURS

1 cup (150 g) cashews

8 ounces (240 g/about 1 generous cup)
soy yogurt (see tip page 183)

1½ teaspoons sea salt

3 tablespoons tapioca flour

1 tablespoon agar agar powder

Our delicious burgers, freshly made pizzas cooked over charcoal, and grilled vegetables naturally taste good without it. But picture yourself serving guests your homemade vegan mozzarella made from a few natural ingredients. They'll be totally amazed.

1. Soak the cashews in water for at least 8 hours. Drain and rinse them well under running water.

2. Combine them with the yogurt, salt and ½ cup (120 ml) water in a blender and process until smooth. Cover and rest the mixture for 24 hours.

3. Mix in the tapioca flour. Dissolve the agar agar in a scant ½ cup (100 ml) water in a saucepan and bring it to a boil over low heat while stirring constantly. Boil for 3 minutes.

4. Add the cashew and yogurt mixture to the pan while stirring constantly and boil over medium heat for 10 minutes.

5. Remove the pan from the heat. Use an ice-cream scoop to make eight to ten mozzarella balls and drop them into a large bowl of ice water. Let cool for 30 minutes, then transfer the balls to a container filled with salted water and refrigerate.

TIP
Our mozzarella can keep for up to 7 days in the refrigerator in an airtight container.

SOFT CORN BREAD

WITH JALAPEÑO

MAKES ONE 9-INCH (23 CM) SQUARE PAN	BAKING TIME 35 MINUTES	PREPARATION TIME 15 MINUTES

4 or 5 jalapeño peppers

2 cups (275 g) cornmeal

1¼ cups (150 g) white spelt flour

1 tablespoon baking powder

1 teaspoon salt

1¼ cups (300 ml) oat milk

¼ cup (50 ml) olive oil

2 teaspoons apple cider vinegar

1. Preheat the oven to 400°F (200°C).

2. Cut the jalapeños into thin rings.

3. Mix all the ingredients together with ⅔ cup (150 ml) water, stirring with a wooden spoon until the flour and liquid combine to form a smooth batter.

4. Pour the batter into a 9-inch (23 cm) square pan lined with parchment paper. Smooth the surface and bake for about 35 minutes.

TIP
Our corn bread with fiery jalapeños goes really well with our craft beer and vegetable chili (page 127).

PICKLED TURNIPS AND CAULIFLOWER

PINK & PUNCHY

MAKES ABOUT 1 POUND (500 G)	**PREPARATION TIME** 15 MINUTES + 1 WEEK

1½ teaspoons salt

1 bay leaf

½ teaspoon black peppercorns

1 large or 2 small turnips
(about 7 ounces/200 g total)

½ medium beet

1 cup (100 g) cauliflower florets

⅓ cup (70 ml) white vinegar

Our pink pickled turnips and cauliflower not only look stylish, but their refreshingly tart and light flavor is an excellent accompaniment to hearty barbecue fare.

1. Bring ½ cup (100 ml) water to a boil with the salt, bay leaf and peppercorns.

2. Peel the turnip and beet and cut into strips 2 cm thick.

3. Layer the vegetables in a clean, sterilized canning jar and fill the jar with the pickling liquid and vinegar.

4. Leave the pink pickles in the refrigerator for 1 week to steep.

TIP
These pickles will keep for one or two months in the fridge. Unopened, they can last much longer at room temperature if properly canned (processed in a hot water bath).

CAMPFIRE TWISTS

BREAD ON A STICK

MAKES 4 TWISTS	BARBECUING TIME 15 MINUTES	PREPARATION TIME 20 MINUTES + 1 HOUR

1 teaspoon (5 g) active dry yeast

1 tablespoon maple syrup

1⅓ cups (170 g) whole-grain spelt flour

3 tablespoons nutritional yeast

1½ teaspoons blue fenugreek seeds or ground coriander

¼ teaspoon salt

This bread simply belongs on an open fire. And whether you're thinking about a campfire or a hot charcoal barbecue, it makes no difference to the taste.

1. Stir the yeast and maple syrup into ½ cup (120 ml) warm water and set aside until the yeast has dissolved.

2. Mix the remaining ingredients together and add the yeast and maple syrup mixture. Stir with a wooden spoon until the flour and liquid combine to form a dough. Knead the dough by hand for 10 minutes on a floured work surface. Put the dough in a bowl, cover and leave in a warm place for 1 hour, or until it has doubled in size.

3. Divide the dough into four uniform pieces. Roll each piece into a long sausage and wind it around a wooden stick or bamboo skewer that has been soaked in water.

4. Bake the twists over indirect heat for 15 minutes, turning them over from time to time.

TIP
The twists will be even more substantial if you add 1 tablespoon each of sunflower seeds, pumpkin seeds and flaxseeds to the dough.

SWEET POTATO BUNS

FOR DELICIOUS BARBECUE BURGERS

MAKES 4 BUNS	BAKING TIME 20 MINUTES	PREPARATION TIME 20 MINUTES + 1 HOUR

FOR THE DOUGH

2 tablespoons ground flaxseeds

One $\frac{1}{4}$-ounce (7 g) packet active dry yeast

1 tablespoon raw cane sugar

2 tablespoons vegan milk

$\frac{1}{2}$ cup (100 g) boiled and mashed sweet potato

2 tablespoons canola oil

2 cups (250 g) white spelt flour

1 teaspoon salt

FOR THE GLAZE

1 tablespoon vegan milk

$1\frac{1}{2}$ teaspoons maple syrup

EXTRAS

1 teaspoon poppy seeds

1. For the dough, mix the flaxseeds with 2 tablespoons water and leave to swell for 10 minutes.

2. Stir the yeast and sugar into $\frac{1}{4}$ cup (60 ml) warm water and the vegan milk and set aside until the yeast has dissolved.

3. Mix the sweet potato with the liquid and oil. In a separate bowl, mix the flour and salt. Add the wet ingredients, including the flaxseed and yeast mixtures, to the dry ones and stir with a wooden spoon. Then turn the dough onto a floured work surface and knead by hand for 10 minutes. Put the dough in a bowl, cover and leave in a warm place for 1 hour, or until it has doubled in size.

4. Divide the dough into four uniform pieces. Lightly press each piece to flatten. Fold the edges inward, turn the pieces upside down and shape them into round buns. Transfer the buns to a baking sheet lined with parchment paper, with their seam (where the sides join) on the underside. Cover and let rise again for another 20 minutes.

5. Preheat the oven to 350°F (180°C).

6. For the glaze, mix the vegan milk and maple syrup together.

7. Brush the burger buns with the maple syrup glaze, sprinkle with the poppy seeds and bake for 20 minutes, or until the tops turns a light golden brown and the buns are fluffy and soft.

HOT PICKLED RADISHES

WITH FRESH JALAPEÑOS

MAKES ABOUT 1 POUND (500 G)	**PREPARATION TIME** 15 MINUTES

11 ounces (300 g) radishes

2 jalapeño peppers

½ cup (100 ml) white vinegar

2 garlic cloves, peeled

3 tablespoons muscovado or dark brown sugar

2 teaspoons dried oregano

1 teaspoon coarse sea salt

¾ teaspoon cumin seeds

1. Thinly slice the radishes and cut the jalapeños into thin rings. Mix the vegetables and put them in a canning jar.

2. Combine the remaining ingredients in a saucepan and bring to a boil. Simmer for 5 minutes.

3. Pour the pickling liquid over the vegetables, close the lid tightly and leave to steep in the refrigerator for at least 2 hours.

TIP
These pickles will keep for one or two months in the fridge. Unopened, they can last much longer at room temperature if properly canned (processed in a hot water bath).

GRILLED CHAPATIS

FOR WRAPS & DIPS

MAKES 6 CHAPATIS	BARBECUING TIME 6 MINUTES	PREPARATION TIME 10 MINUTES + 20 MINUTES

$1\frac{2}{3}$ cups (200 g) all-purpose flour

$\frac{1}{2}$ teaspoon salt

3 tablespoons canola oil

1. Mix all the ingredients together with $\frac{1}{2}$ cup (100 ml) water, stirring with a wooden spoon until the flour and liquid combine to form a dough. Turn the dough out onto a floured work surface and knead it by hand for 5 minutes. Cover the dough and rest it for 20 minutes.

2. Divide the dough into six uniform pieces and roll them out as thinly as possible with a rolling pin.

3. Grill them over direct heat for 2 to 3 minutes each side.

TIP

Our chapatis go together deliciously with our tandoori tofu skewers (page 71) and seitan shish kebab wraps (page 135).

INDEX

INDEX

MANY THANKS!

Hey blog readers, are you still there? As always, our warmest thanks go to you.
Where would we be without you?

Many thanks again to Kristina and Walter from Neunzehn Verlag.
It was a great pleasure for us to work with you again.

Once again a big high five goes out to all vegans and animal rights workers
for your commitment and efforts.

Thanks to Nessa for turning our mumblings into beautiful explanatory drawings.

And of course, a big thank you goes to our parents, families and friends.

And last but not least, heartfelt thanks to you, dear reader.